RAISING
WINNING
STUDENTS

How To Guarantee Your Child
Will Succeed In School

A Field Manual for 21st Century Parenting

THE
PARENTS
UNION

© 2012 by The Parents Union
1416 112th Ave. NE
Bellevue, Washington 98004

All rights reserved.

Front cover concept by 206inc.
Book design by Lightbourne, Inc.

ISBN 978-1-939207-01-2

CONTENTS

America's K–12 public schools are in crisis. Too many of our children are not graduating from high school. And too many of those who do graduate are unprepared for college and careers.

It seems that many groups are attempting to tackle the problem, from Congress to teachers' unions. But how does that help your child today? The truth is that it probably doesn't. Although systemic and earth-shaking reform is badly needed in our school system, such change doesn't happen overnight.

WHAT MAKES THE GREATEST DIFFERENCE TODAY IN YOUR CHILD'S EDUCATION IS YOU, THE PARENT OR CAREGIVER.

I believe strongly that we must re-engage parents in the education of their children. The biggest impact of parents occurs in the child's earliest years, before pre-school. The clear reality, however, is that your involvement is needed from the cradle through high school graduation and beyond.

I also believe we need to make learning fun, a constant adventure where young, malleable minds expand to explore history, science, the arts, nature, relationships, and worlds that are of interest. Second, we need to make learning personal. Last, we need to arm each student with the feeling of being empowered to pursue his or her individual goals in life.

Perhaps you feel you have little individual power to make sense out of where to attack the problem of enabling your child to get the best possible education. Even those parents who have the economic means to enroll their children in private schools may feel overwhelmed by the many-headed creature that is the school system. The questions and issues are endless:

What are your choices?

How do you recognize good schools?

More to the point, how can you tell a school is right for your child?

What defines a great teacher?

How are schools organized, and to whom do you talk with when your child is having difficulty?

The best way to tackle these issues is 1) one at a time, and 2) never give up.

The book you are now reading, *Raising Winning Students: A Field Manual for 21ˢᵗ Century Parenting*, has been constructed for you, the parent—the single most influential person in your child's education. This book is your personal key to help unlock the potential of the school system for your child.

It is fitting that the last chapter addresses advocacy, because once you open educational doors for your own child, it is a natural leap to use the skills and knowledge and connections you've gained to help other parents and other children.

In my book *Outrageous Learning*, published in 2009, I described one approach to grappling with school improvement, whether for a single student or all students, and to do so in a way that "energizes all stakeholders":

> The Japanese are largely credited with focusing on the benefits of long-term, continuous process improvement throughout all aspects of life. It all started with Toyota during the rebuilding of Japan after World War II. Kaizen (literally, "change to become good") is an original Japanese management concept for incremental, gradual and continuous improvement. Toyota Motors is world

renowned for making Kaizen an integral part of its corporate culture. I believe the education industry would benefit greatly by applying Kaizen concepts.

Kaizen is a system that can involve everyone within the school district or school, as well as many external stakeholders. The beauty of Kaizen is that it does not rely on one big, audacious catalytic element for systemic change, or even on 11 planks of some book. Instead, it relies on the long-term view of encouraging everyone to participate in making small improvement suggestions, frequently and regularly.

Small, continuous improvement, applied assiduously by all stakeholders, can eventually lead to substantial change. Consideration should also be given to using Kaizen Blitz, a more concentrated form that focuses significant resources on a limited and narrowly defined objective. (p. 91)

Changing the education system in America will take time. But changing your child's educational experience can happen quickly.

I founded The Parents Union because I deeply believe that every child is entitled to the highest quality education possible that prepares him or her for a successful and contributive life. I urge you to become a true partner in your child's education and to lead the way as an advocate for all children's educational success. *Raising Winning Students* is your key.

September 2012
SCOTT OKI
Founder/Chairman
The Parents Union

INTRODUCTION

You hold in your hands a remarkable resource—the first parenting guide by parents for parents. More than twenty-five top authors and experts have contributed to what we call our *Field Manual for 21st Century Parenting*. Our goal is nothing less than to provide you with a one-stop resource that will help you ensure that your child will succeed in school and in life.

That's a pretty tall order. For our kids to succeed in school and in life there are many elements that come into play. First and foremost are our intentional, directed and consistent efforts as parents. Many experts will tell you that parents are their children's first teacher. And as we travel down the path of life, we continue to teach our children about values, about resilience, about faith and effort, and ultimately life and death.

It's no wonder that many parents have exclaimed in exasperation, "There's an owner's manual for my car and my computer—why isn't there one for my kid?" Many of us just don't feel prepared for parenting. It can be mysterious and overwhelming.

And sometimes kids just show up—through marriage, divorce, family changes, and unexpected pregnancies. No matter how they come into our lives, we have to face the fact that we are their parents, and we need a plan for their healthy growth, their development and their education.

This guidebook was created to help you make those plans and to carry them out in ways that lead to a joyful family and a successful education. Our goal is to help you become a true partner in your child's education so that a holistic environment can be created both in and out of school that provides the best insurance that your child will become a winner.

ABOUT THE PARENTS UNION

The Parents Union is the first statewide organization by parents, for parents and families dedicated to ensuring that each and every child in Washington State graduates with the skills to achieve their dreams. We believe that every child can learn and every school can be successful. Our organization is focused on values starting with the belief that our education system should be transparent and performance driven, and everyone, beginning with parents, should hold ourselves accountable for what we say, what we do and how we spend the money.

These simple core beliefs—transparency, accountability and performance-driven systems, plus an unshakable belief in the potential of all children and a commitment to their happiness, healthy growth, development and future success, are the bedrock convictions that we believe are needed to transform our education system in Washington state and throughout our nation.

If you are not already a member, we urge you to join us. Go to www.theparentsunion.org to become part of the growing movement of engaged and empowered parents and families.

HOW TO USE THIS GUIDEBOOK

Raising Winning Students is organized so you can find answers to questions you need quickly. While many parenting books are long on philosophy—and there's nothing wrong with that—this guidebook is focused on identifying your problem or question, providing you with checklists and resources to understand your unique situation, and putting action items at your fingertips to begin solving the issue today. The Table of Contents and Index have been created to help you navigate more than 200 pages of content from our contributors.

You can also use this guidebook to take you on a specific journey—a journey that starts with understanding your own school and learning experience, your expectations for your children and gaining insights to how each of your children learns. Working through these aspects will help you become a true partner with your child's teachers, counselors, tutors, coaches and school leaders.

Learning is a lifelong process. As parents, we are always learning—from our friends, from our elders, from experts and from our kids. At The Parents Union, we are always learning, too. We learn from researchers and experts, from educators and academics, and most of all we learn from you, our members. Help us make this the most valuable resource possible for all parents. Let us know what you think. If you tried something you learned in this guidebook and it worked well, send us an email. If it didn't work, let us know that as well and how you think we might improve this resource. Send emails to editor@theparentsunion.org and feel free to share your thoughts on our online forum at www.theparentsunion.org/forum.

It is our greatest hope that you experience the joy of helping your children become winning students.

This is the beginning of something great!

MARC SACHNOFF
CEO/Chief Parent
Editor

1

THE POWER OF PARENT ENGAGEMENT:

Your Impact on Your Student, Your School, Your Community

ANNE HENDERSON, senior consultant, Community Organizing and Engagement at the Annenberg Institute for School Reform, is a national treasure. She is the "godmother" of parent empowerment in America and has been crusading on behalf of all parents and their children for thirty years. Anne's work has informed a lot of how we envision The Parents Union and its membership will impact education on the school and classroom level. In this important piece, Anne talks about the role of "demand parents." There's nothing wrong with wanting to be involved and pressing—politely but firmly—for answers to questions impacting your child's education until you get satisfaction.

—Marc Sachnoff, Chief Parent, The Parents Union

WHY PARTNER WITH YOUR CHILD'S SCHOOL?

ANNE T. HENDERSON

The benefits to partnering with your child's school are significant: Students whose parents are engaged in their education tend to do better, stay in school longer, enjoy school more, and go on to higher education.

This is true no matter what the educational level or income of the family, even when other problems are part of the mix. When students feel that their family "has their back," it's reflected in better grades, attitudes, behavior, adjustment to school, and willingness to take on more challenging work.

That's what I hear when I talk with young people: They want their parents to know what they're doing and to back them up.

It's clear that many parents find it hard to step up or to know what to do. They are beset, first, by all the many demands on their time—including work and other family obligations—and second, by schools that send messages basically saying, "Don't interfere; we know what we're doing."

Schools also tend to connect directly with students and often leave parents out of the loop. But if parents are out of the loop, there is no loop! How do parents find out how to navigate the educational system and take advantage of the opportunities that are available for their children?

"DEMAND PARENTS"

To bridge that gap, it's important for parents to know what actions they can take that are most productive. Dr. Rudy Crew, author of *Only Connect: The Way to Save Our Schools*, ran two of the four largest school districts in the United States—New York City and Miami-Dade County—before becoming professor of clinical education at the University of Southern California. He also serves on President Barack Obama's Education Policy Council.

Parents, Crew says, need to know how to be "demand parents," parents who "demand things from their schools because they understand that they are indeed owed something and it is their responsibility to get it for their children" (Crewe, Only Connect, p. 155). Dr. Crew's approach is rooted in his upbringing and his own parents, who went to battle for him as a student. Before parents can be effective advocates, however, they must educate themselves about their children's needs and the resources of the school system. This also implies that parents are responsible for making sure their children go to school and are on time, attend class, do their schoolwork, and understand the material covered.

Parents must know how to be proactive and how to stand up for their children. They should be kept informed about how their children are doing, but schools tend to not do that. The more that schools feel this demand, the more they will respond. The results will come, just as they do in supply-and-demand economics.

Where do parents learn how to do that? Most of the time, they either learn from their own parents who did that, or they might have friends who are "demand parents" and who coach them. Schools are not prepared to show them how, nor are they especially interested in creating parents who make demands!

Another resource for gaining these skills is the parent organization at individual schools.

PARENT ORGANIZATIONS

This repositions the role of the parent organization. Traditionally, the role of parent organizations has been to support parents help students at home and to organize volunteers for the school. Those roles must be expanded to include teaching parents to be proactive in helping schools reach their improvement goals. Nationwide, we have major goals, and they won't happen until parents become full partners. In schools where this happens, schools invariably improve.

The No Child Left Behind Act, passed by the U.S. Congress in 2001, supports standards-based education reform based on the premise that high standards and measurable goals can improve individual outcomes in education. The result? Schools are under the gun to improve. They are desperate to look better and do better. If schools understand that parents want to help and can deliver, it's a game-changer.

Parents don't have to be experts in school reform to make a difference. What they need to do is ask the right questions. It takes self-confidence, even what my father called "moxie," to ask a teacher tough questions. I don't mean to confront a teacher combatively, but to pursue a line of productive inquiry. For example: "You say that my child is behind in math skills. What are you doing to catch my child up? Can you give me some ideas how to help at home? How long will it take for her to catch up? Will he be eligible to be in the pre-algebra class next year if we work together on this?"

It's important that the parent organization at every school represent all parents, not just a single social or economic group. Every parent organization should be prepared to reach out to those who need encouragement to step up—for example, sharing data such as the target skills students that should be learning at each level—and coaching parents how to be "demand parents."

The overriding purpose of parent organizations must be to help the school reach its improvement goals. Those goals should be plastered everywhere, for every grade, and in every classroom. Everyone—parents, teachers, students, administrators—should know what the goals are, what the school is doing to achieve them, and what progress the students are making. Organizing regular "state of the school" meetings is a good strategy for keeping the goals firmly in focus.

BEYOND HIGH SCHOOL

In our global economy, all students will need to have post-secondary education that will prepare them for a career. Without a college or technical education after high school, well-paying job prospects will be severely limited. Parents must be aware of this and understand that if their children aren't reading proficiently by the end of third grade, their future success in school is likewise limited. In fact, the biggest predictor of success in education is the student's skill level at kindergarten.

Another benefit of the partnership between parents and schools: It builds the capacity of families to support children over the long haul, all the way to the workplace, by being a smarter consumer, knowing the right questions to ask, and how to understand the system.

WHAT CAN YOU DO?

You're a parent, and that means you're busy. What are the most effective actions you can take?

1. *If you can only do one thing to help your child get a better education, it's to build a relationship with your child's teachers.* That's easier in elementary school. If your child is in middle or high school, with several teachers, reach out to a homeroom teacher or advisor. Get to know him or her and give that person the opportunity to know you.

    Teachers have higher expectations of students whose parents they know. Teachers typically have 25–30 students. They may only know half the families. Parents can take the initiative in making sure they are one of those families.

2. Join the parent organization at your child's school. There is strength in numbers. If you raise an issue alone—perhaps children are being bullied at school, or lunches are not sufficiently nutritious—schools will tend to discount lone voices. But if you are one of five parents voicing your concern, they're far more likely to listen and take action.

    Perhaps your school does not even have a parent organization. Start one. The National PTA (http://www.pta.org) offers support and resources to kickstart your efforts, but don't stop there.

(Editor's Note: The Parents Union *is also a good starting place to find the tools and resources to build an effective parent organization.)*

FOUR LEVELS OF PARTNERSHIP

(Adapted from *Beyond the Bake Sale*)

Ask yourself: what might a school look like that has created a genuine culture of school-family-community partnership, and that has made real progress toward high social and academic achievement for all students?

Consider four levels of partnership:

- **Partnership School**
- **Open-Door School**
- **Come-If-We-Call School**
- **Fortress School**

How can you tell where your school is at? Use the scoring guides that follow

PARTNERSHIP SCHOOL

All families and communities have something great to offer—we do whatever it takes to work closely together to make sure every single student succeeds.

Building Relationships

- ☐ Family center is always open, full of interesting learning materials to borrow
- ☐ Home visits are made to every new family
- ☐ Activities honor families' contributions
- ☐ Building is open to community use and social services are available to families

Linking to Learning

- All family activities connect to what students are learning
- Parents and teachers look at student work and test results together
- Community groups offer tutoring and homework programs at the school
- Students' work goes home every week, with a scoring guide

Addressing Differences

- Translators are readily available
- Teachers use books and materials about families' cultures
- PTA includes all families
- Local groups help staff reach parents

Supporting Advocacy

- There is a clear, open process for resolving problems
- Teachers contact families each month to discuss student progress
- Student-led parent-teacher conferences are held three times a year for thirty minutes

Sharing Power

- Parents and teachers research issues such as prejudice and tracking
- Parent group is focused on improving student achievement
- Families are involved in all major decisions
- Parents can use the school's phone, copier, fax, and computers
- Staff work with local organizers to improve the school and neighborhood

OPEN-DOOR SCHOOL

Parents can be involved at our school in many ways—we're working hard to get an even bigger turnout for our activities. When we ask the community to help, people often respond.

Building Relationships

☐ Teachers contact families once a year

☐ Parent coordinator is available if families have questions or need help

☐ Office staff are friendly

☐ Staff contact community agencies and organizations when help is needed

Linking to Learning

☐ Teachers explain test scores if asked

☐ Folders of student work go home occasionally

☐ School holds curriculum nights three or four times a year

☐ Staff let families know about out-of-school classes in the community

Addressing Differences

☐ Office staff will find a translator if parents ask in advance

☐ Multicultural nights are held once a year

☐ "Minority" parents have their own group

Supporting Advocacy

☐ Principal will meet with parents to discuss a problem

☐ Regular progress reports go to parents, but test data can be hard to understand

☐ Parent-teacher conferences are held twice a year

Sharing Power

☐ Parents can raise issues at PTA meetings or see the principal

☐ Parent group sets its own agenda and raises money for the school

☐ Resource center for low-income families is housed in a portable classroom next to the school

☐ PTA officers can use the school office

☐ A community representative sits on the school council

COME-IF-WE-CALL SCHOOL

Parents are welcome when we ask them, but there's only so much they can offer. The most important thing they can do is to help their kids at home. We know where to get help in the community if we need it.

Building Relationships

☐ Better-educated parents are more involved

☐ "Many immigrant parents don't have time to come or contribute"

☐ Staff are very selective about who comes into the school

Linking to Learning

☐ Parents are told what students will be learning at the fall open house

☐ Parents can call the office to get teacher-recorded messages about homework

☐ Workshops are offered on parenting

Addressing Differences

- ☐ "We can't deal with twenty different languages"
- ☐ "Parents can bring a translator with them"
- ☐ "This school just isn't the same as it used to be"

Supporting Advocacy

- ☐ School calls families when children have problems
- ☐ Families visit school on report card pickup day and can see a teacher if they call first

Sharing Power

- ☐ Principal sets agenda for parent meetings
- ☐ PTA gets the school's message out
- ☐ "Parents are not experts in education"
- ☐ Community groups can address the school board if they have concerns

FORTRESS SCHOOL

Parents belong at home, not at school. If students don't do well, it's because their families don't give them enough support. We're already doing all we can. Our school is an oasis in a troubled community. We want to keep it that way.

Building Relationships

- ☐ Families do not "bother" school staff
- ☐ "Minority families don't value education"
- ☐ Parents need security clearance to come in
- ☐ It is important to keep community influences out of the school

Linking to Learning

- ☐ Curriculum and standards are considered too complex for parents to understand
- ☐ "If parents want more information, they can ask for it"
- ☐ "We're teachers, not social workers"

Addressing Differences

- ☐ "Those parents need to learn English"
- ☐ "We teach about our country—that's what those parents need to know"
- ☐ "This neighborhood is going downhill"

Supporting Advocacy

- ☐ Parents don't come to conferences
- ☐ Problems are dealt with by the professional staff
- ☐ Teachers don't feel safe with parents

Sharing Power

- ☐ Principal picks a small group of "cooperative parents" to help out
- ☐ Families are afraid to complain: "They might take it out on my kid"
- ☐ "Community groups should mind their own business; they don't know about education"

WHERE DOES YOUR SCHOOL FALL?

Check the boxes that have the most statements under them marked or circled. Check only one box in a row.

- If three or more of your checked boxes fall in the Fortress School section and none under Open-Door or Partnership, your school is trying to keep parents away rather than work with them. In standards-based terms, it is **below basic.**

- If three or more of your checked boxes fall under Come-if-We-Call and none under Partnership, your school may want parents to be involved only on its terms. In standards-based terms, it is at the **basic** level.

- If at least four of your checked boxes fall under Open-Door or Partnership and none are under Fortress School, your school welcomes families and supports them to be involved in a number of ways. In standards-based terms, it is **proficient.**

- If at least three of your checked boxes are under Partnership and the rest are under Open-Door, your school is willing and able to work with all families. We bet the student achievement level goes up every year. In standards-based terms, it is **advanced.**

For more information, consider:

- Dr. Rudy Crew, *Only Connect: The Way to Save Our Schools*,

- National PTA (http://www.pta.org)

- Henderson, Mapp, Johnson and Davies (2007), *Beyond the Bake Sale: The Essential Guide to Family-School Partnerships* (NY: The New Press)

ANNE T. HENDERSON *is senior consultant to the Annenberg Institute for School Reform, and author of many books, reports, article and tools about engaging families to improve student achievement.*

Teacher and education gadfly **ALFIE KOHN** provides us with a great place to begin this 21st century field guide to parenting. If our goal in The Parents Union is to provide a world-class education for each and every child in Washington State, then we have to ask the questions: What is a world class education? What is the purpose of education? And what does it mean to be well educated?

Is the purpose of the thirteen-plus years of schooling that we subject our kids to supposed to be about the accumulation of facts and skills and test scores? Or is it, as Alfie suggests in this thoroughly provoking piece, a learning process centered around problems, projects, and questions?

This may seem like a heady discussion, but it's worthwhile for us as parents to take the time to ask ourselves these questions. At The Parents Union we believe that education should be focused on the happiness, healthy growth and development and future success of every child. I don't know a lot of schools that are presently focused on these outcomes. Rather most schools seem to be focused on high stakes testing outcomes and what Alfie calls the "Bunch o' Facts" model.

And worthy also of our consideration is the quote from Nel Noddings, professor emerita at Stanford University. In Alfie's piece, Professor Noddings, urges us to reject "the deadly notion that the schools' first priority should be intellectual development" and contends that "the main aim of education should be to produce competent, caring, loving, and lovable people."

—Marc Sachnoff, Chief Parent, The Parents Union

WHAT DOES IT MEAN TO BE WELL-EDUCATED?

BY ALFIE KOHN

(www.alfiekohn.org/teaching/welleducated.htm)

No one should offer pronouncements about what it means to be well-educated without meeting my wife. When I met Alisa, she was at Harvard, putting the finishing touches on her doctoral dissertation in anthropology. A year later, having spent her entire life in school, she decided to do the only logical thing . . . and apply to medical school. Today she is a practicing physician—and an excellent one at that, judging by feedback from her patients and colleagues.

She will, however, freeze up if you ask her what 8 times 7 is, because she never learned the multiplication table. And forget about grammar ("Me and him went over her house today" is fairly typical) or literature ("Who's Faulkner?"). After a dozen years, I continue to be impressed on a regular basis by the agility of her mind as well as by how much she doesn't know. (I'm also bowled over by what a wonderful person she is, but that's beside the point.)

So what do you make of this paradox with whom I live? Is she a walking indictment of the system that let her get so far—twenty-nine years of schooling, not counting medical residency—without acquiring the basics of English and math? Or does she offer an invitation to rethink what it means to be well-educated since what she lacks hasn't prevented her from being a deep-thinking, high-functioning, multi-credentialed, professionally successful individual?

Of course, if those features describe what it means to be well-educated, then there is no dilemma to be resolved. She fits the bill. The problem arises only if your definition includes a list of facts and skills that one must have but that she lacks. In that case, though, my wife is not alone. Thanks to the Internet, which allows writers and researchers to circulate rough drafts of their manuscripts, I've come to realize just how many truly brilliant people cannot spell or punctuate. Their insights and discoveries may be changing the shape of their respective fields, but they can't use an apostrophe correctly to save their lives.

Or what about me (he suddenly inquired, relinquishing his comfortable perch from which issue all those judgments of other people)? I could embarrass myself pretty quickly by listing the number of classic works of literature I've never read. And I can multiply reasonably well, but everything mathematical I was taught after first-year algebra (and even some of that) is completely gone. How well-educated am I?

■　■　■

The issue is sufficiently complex that questions are easier to formulate than answers. So let's at least be sure we're asking the right questions and framing them well.

1. **The Point of Schooling:** Rather than attempting to define what it means to be well-educated, should we instead be asking about the *purposes of education*? The latter formulation invites us to look beyond academic goals. For example, Nel Noddings, professor emerita at Stanford University, urges us to reject "the deadly notion that the schools' first priority should be intellectual development" and contends that "the main aim of education should be to produce competent, caring, loving, and lovable people." Alternatively, we might wade into the dispute between those who see education as a means to creating or sustaining a democratic society and those who believe its primary role is economic, amounting to an "investment" in

future workers and, ultimately, corporate profits. In short, perhaps the question "How do we know if education has been successful?" shouldn't be posed until we have asked what it's supposed to be successful at.

2. **Evaluating People vs. Their Education:** Does the phrase *well-educated* refer to a quality of the schooling you received, or to something about you? Does it denote what you were taught, or what you learned (and remember)? If the term applies to what you now know and can do, you could be poorly educated despite having received a top-notch education. However, if the term refers to the quality of your schooling, then we'd have to conclude that a lot of "well-educated" people sat through lessons that barely registered, or at least are hazy to the point of irrelevance a few years later.

3. **An Absence of Consensus:** Is it even possible to agree on a *single definition* of what every high school student should know or be able to do in order to be considered well-educated? Is such a definition expected to remain invariant across cultures (with a single standard for the U.S. and Somalia, for example), or even across subcultures (South-Central Los Angeles and Scarsdale; a Louisiana fishing community, the upper East side of Manhattan, and Pennsylvania Dutch country)? How about across historical eras: would anyone seriously argue that our criteria for "well-educated" today are exactly the same as those used a century ago—or that they should be?

   To cast a skeptical eye on such claims is not necessarily to suggest that the term is purely relativistic: you like vanilla, I like chocolate; you favor knowledge about poetry, I prefer familiarity with the Gettysburg Address. Some criteria are more defensible than others. Nevertheless, we have to acknowledge a striking absence of consensus about what the term ought to mean. Furthermore, any consensus that does develop is ineluctably rooted in time and place. It is misleading and even dangerous to justify our own pedagogical values by pretending they are grounded in some objective, transcendent Truth, as though the quality of being well-educated is a Platonic form waiting to be discovered.

4. **Some Poor Definitions:** Should we instead try to stipulate which answers *don't* make sense? I'd argue that certain attributes are either insufficient (possessing them isn't enough to make one well-educated) or unnecessary (one can be well-educated without possessing them)—or both. Let us therefore consider ruling out:

   Seat time. Merely sitting in classrooms for x hours doesn't make one well-educated.

   Job skills. It would be a mistake to reduce schooling to vocational preparation, if only because we can easily imagine graduates who are well-prepared for the workplace (or at least for some workplaces) but whom we would not regard as well-educated. In any case, pressure to redesign secondary education so as to suit the demands of employers reflects little more than the financial interests—and the political power—of these corporations.

   Test scores. To a disconcerting extent, high scores on standardized tests signify a facility with taking standardized tests. Most teachers can instantly name students who are talented thinkers but who just don't do well on these exams—as well as students whose scores seem to overestimate their intellectual gifts. Indeed, researchers have found a statistically significant correlation between high scores on a range of standardized tests and a shallow approach to learning. In any case, no single test is sufficiently valid, reliable, or meaningful that it can be treated as a marker for academic success.

Memorization of a bunch o' facts. Familiarity with a list of words, names, books, and ideas is a uniquely poor way to judge who is well-educated. As the philosopher Alfred North Whitehead observed long ago, "A merely well-informed man is the most useless bore on God's earth. . . . Scraps of information" are only worth something if they are put to use, or at least "thrown into fresh combinations."

Look more carefully at the superficially plausible claim that you must be familiar with, say, *King Lear* in order to be considered well-educated. To be sure, it's a classic meditation on mortality, greed, belated understanding, and other important themes. But *how* familiar with it must you be? Is it enough that you can name its author, or that you know it's a play? Do you have to be able to recite the basic plot? What if you read it once but barely remember it now?

If you don't like that example, pick another one. How much do you have to know about neutrinos, or the Boxer rebellion, or the side-angle-side theorem? If deep understanding is required, then (a) very few people could be considered well-educated (which raises serious doubts about the reasonableness of such a definition), and (b) the number of items about which anyone could have that level of knowledge is sharply limited because time is finite. On the other hand, how can we justify a cocktail-party level of familiarity with all these items—reminiscent of Woody Allen's summary of *War and Peace* after taking a speed-reading course: "It's about Russia." What sense does it make to say that one person is well-educated for having a single sentence's worth of knowledge about the Progressive Era or photosynthesis, while someone who has to look it up is not?

Knowing a lot of stuff may seem harmless, albeit insufficient, but the problem is that efforts to shape schooling around this goal, dressed up with pretentious labels like "cultural literacy," have the effect of taking time away from more meaningful objectives, such as knowing how to think. If the Bunch o' Facts model proves a poor foundation on which to decide who is properly educated, it makes no sense to peel off items from such a list and assign clusters of them to students at each grade level. It is as poor a basis for designing curriculum as it is for judging the success of schooling.

The number of people who do, in fact, confuse the possession of a storehouse of knowledge with being "smart" —the latter being a disconcertingly common designation for those who fare well on quiz shows—is testament to the naïve appeal that such a model holds. But there are also political implications to be considered here. To emphasize the importance of absorbing a pile of information is to support a larger worldview that sees the primary purpose of education as reproducing our current culture. It is probably not a coincidence that a Core Knowledge model wins rave reviews from Phyllis Schlafly's Eagle Forum (and other conservative Christian groups) as well as from the likes of *Investor's Business Daily*. To be sure, not every individual who favors this approach is a right-winger, but defining the notion of educational mastery in terms of the number of facts one can recall is well-suited to the task of preserving the status quo. By contrast, consider Dewey's suggestion that an educated person is one who has "gained the power of reflective attention, the power to hold problems, questions, before the mind." Without this capability, he added, "the mind remains at the mercy of custom and external suggestions."

5. **Mandating a Single Definition:** *Who gets to decide* what it means to be well-educated? Even assuming that you

and I agree to include one criterion and exclude another, that doesn't mean our definition should be imposed with the force of law—taking the form, for example, of requirements for a high school diploma. There are other considerations, such as the real suffering imposed on individuals who aren't permitted to graduate from high school, the egregious disparities in resources and opportunities available in different neighborhoods, and so on.

More to the point, the fact that so many of us *don't* agree suggests that a national (or, better yet, international) conversation should continue, that one definition may never fit all, and, therefore, that we should leave it up to local communities to decide who gets to graduate. But that is not what has happened. In about half the states, people sitting atop Mount Olympus have decreed that anyone who doesn't pass a certain standardized test will be denied a diploma and, by implication, classified as inadequately educated. This example of accountability gone haywire violates not only common sense but the consensus of educational measurement specialists. And the consequences are entirely predictable: no high school graduation for a disproportionate number of students of color, from low-income neighborhoods, with learning disabilities, attending vocational schools, or not yet fluent in English.

Less obviously, the idea of making diplomas contingent on passing an exam answers by default the question of what it means to be well- (or sufficiently) educated: Rather than grappling with the messy issues involved, we simply declare that standardized tests will tell us the answer. This is disturbing not merely because of the inherent limits of the tests, but also because teaching becomes distorted when passing those tests becomes the paramount goal. Students arguably receive an inferior education when pressure is applied to raise their test scores, which means that high school exit exams may actually *lower* standards.

Beyond proclaiming "Pass this standardized test or you don't graduate," most states now issue long lists of curriculum standards, containing hundreds of facts, skills, and subskills that all students are expected to master at a given grade level and for a given subject. These standards are not guidelines but mandates (to which teachers are supposed to "align" their instruction). In effect, a Core Knowledge model, with its implication of students as interchangeable receptacles into which knowledge is poured, has become the law of the land in many places. Surely even defenders of this approach can appreciate the difference between *arguing* in its behalf and *requiring* that every school adopt it.

6. **The Good School:** Finally, instead of asking what it means to be well-educated, perhaps we should inquire into the *qualities* of a school likely to offer a good education. I've offered my own answer to that question at book length, as have other contributors to this issue. As I see it, the best sort of schooling is organized around problems, projects, and questions—as opposed to facts, skills, and disciplines. Knowledge is acquired, of course, but in a context and for a purpose. The emphasis is not only on depth rather than breadth, but also on discovering ideas rather than on covering a prescribed curriculum. Teachers are generalists first and specialists (in a given subject matter) second; they commonly collaborate to offer interdisciplinary courses that students play an active role in designing. All of this happens in small, democratic schools that are experienced as caring communities.

    Notwithstanding the claims of traditionalists eager to offer—and then dismiss—a touchy-feely caricature of progressive education, a substantial body of evidence exists to support the effectiveness of each of these components as well as the benefits of using them in combination. By contrast, it isn't easy to find *any* data to justify the traditional (and still dominant) model of secondary education: large schools, short classes, huge student loads for each teacher, a fact-transmission kind of instruction that is the very antithesis of "student-centered," the virtual absence of any attempt to integrate diverse areas of study, the rating and ranking of students, and so on. Such a system acts as a powerful *obstacle* to good teaching, and it thwarts the best efforts of many talented educators on a daily basis.

Low-quality instruction can be assessed with low-quality tests, including homegrown quizzes and standardized exams designed to measure (with faux objectivity) the number of facts and skills crammed into short-term memory. The effects of high-quality instruction are trickier, but not impossible, to assess. The most promising model turns on the notion of "exhibitions" of learning, in which students reveal their understanding by means of in-depth projects, portfolios of assignments, and other demonstrations—a model pioneered by Ted Sizer, Deborah Meier, and others affiliated with the Coalition of Essential Schools. By now we're fortunate to have access not only to essays about how this might be done (such as Sizer's invaluable *Horace* series) but to books about schools that are actually doing it: *The Power of Their Ideas* by Meier, about Central Park East Secondary School in New York City; *Rethinking High School* by Harvey Daniels and his colleagues, about Best Practice High School in Chicago; and *One Kid at a Time* by Eliot Levine, about the Met in Providence, RI.

The assessments in such schools are based on meaningful standards of excellence, standards that may collectively offer the best answer to our original question simply because to meet those criteria is as good a way as any to show that one is well-educated. The Met School focuses on social reasoning, empirical reasoning, quantitative reasoning, communication, and personal qualities (such as responsibility, capacity for leadership, and self-awareness). Meier has emphasized the importance of developing five "habits of mind": the value of raising questions about *evidence* ("How do we know what we know?"), *point of view* ("Whose perspective does this represent?"), *connections* ("How is this related to that?"), *supposition* ("How might things have been otherwise?"), and *relevance* ("Why is this important?").

It's not only the ability to raise and answer those questions that matters, though, but also the disposition to do so. For that matter, any set of intellectual objectives, any description of what it means to think deeply and critically, should be accompanied by a reference to one's interest or intrinsic motivation to do such thinking. Dewey reminded us that the goal of education is more education. To be well-educated, then, is to have the desire as well as the means to make sure that learning never ends.

2

IT STARTS WITH ME

A Parental Journey of Self-assessment

As parents we all want our children to have a strong character. We want them to know right from wrong, be people who can love others and are loveable. We want them to be aware of their strengths and have the capability to overcome their weaknesses. But in order to help our children we first need to understand our own character strengths. In this piece Psychologist, **DR. RYAN M. NIEMIEC** Education Director at the non-profit VIA Institute on Character, shows you how to indentify your core character strengths. There's even a free online assessment test.

—Marc Sachnoff, Chief Parent, The Parents Union

THE CHARACTER STRENGTHS OF PARENTS

RYAN M. NIEMIEC, PSY.D.

Education Director, VIA Institute on Character

- Who are *you* at your core?
- What are your *highest* strengths?
- What internal qualities do you have that you could bring forth *most* strongly into this world? Into your journey as a parent?

Raising a child with strong character starts with ourselves. How can we expect to know our child if we don't know ourselves well? How might we help our child when we are unable to help ourselves?

The following chart reviews a "common language" for understanding our best qualities. This chart depicts the VIA Classification which outlines 24 character strengths that have been found to be universal across cultures, nations, and beliefs.

THE VIA CLASSIFICATION OF CHARACTER STRENGTHS AND VIRTUES

THE VIRTUE OF WISDOM (thinking-type strengths that help acquire and use knowledge)

Creativity: Original; adaptive; ingenuity

Curiosity: Interest; novelty-seeking; exploration; openness to experience

Judgment: Critical thinking; thinking things through; open-minded

Love of Learning: Mastering new skills & topics; systematically adding to knowledge

Perspective: Wisdom; providing wise counsel; taking the big picture view

THE VIRTUE OF COURAGE (emotional strengths that help us face opposition and challenge)

Bravery: Valor; not shrinking from fear; speaking up for what's right

Perseverance: Persistence; industry; finishing what one starts

Honesty: Authenticity; integrity

Zest: Vitality; enthusiasm; vigor; energy; feeling alive and activated

THE VIRTUE OF HUMANITY (interpersonal strengths that helps tend and befriend others)

Love: Both loving and being loved; valuing close relations with others

Kindness: Generosity; nurturance; care; compassion; altruism; "niceness"

Social Intelligence: Aware of the motives/feelings of oneself & others

THE VIRTUE OF JUSTICE (civic strengths that help us build a healthy community)

Teamwork: Citizenship; social responsibility; loyalty

Fairness: Just; not letting feelings bias decisions about others

Leadership: Organizing group activities; encouraging a group to get things done

THE VIRTUE OF TEMPERANCE (self-control strengths that protect us from vices)

Forgiveness: Mercy; accepting others' shortcomings; giving people a second chance

Humility: Modesty; letting one's accomplishments speak for themselves

Prudence: Careful; cautious; not taking undue risks

Self-Regulation: Self-control; disciplined; managing impulses & emotions

THE VIRTUE OF TRANSCENDENCE (spiritual strengths that help us connect with the larger universe)

Appreciation of Beauty and Excellence: Awe; wonder; elevation

Gratitude: Thankful for the good; expressing thanks; feeling blessed

Hope: Optimism; future-mindedness; future orientation

Humor: Playfulness; bringing smiles to others; lighthearted

Spirituality: Religiousness; faith; purpose; meaning

Working with Your Strengths

Here's a quick, three-step process for working with your character strengths:

1. **Aware**
2. **Explore**
3. **Apply**

It's that easy! Let's go through each phase:

PHASE 1: AWARE

All change begins with awareness. Most people are not aware of their best qualities, and those that are aware may readily take their strengths for granted. Simply asking yourself the question—what are my highest character strengths? – will help you move in the right direction. As you put your attention on your strengths you will be cultivating a general self-awareness, also called mindfulness.

Signature Strengths

You have and express each of the 24 character strengths. However, some strengths are more central to your identity and are called signature strengths. More specifically, a signature strength is:

- Natural and easy for you to express

- Energizing and uplifting

- Authentic and feels like the "real you"

- Expressed strongly across all domains of your life (e.g., family, work, social)

- Nominated by others as one of your highest strengths

Example: Mary Jane is the parent of two young children. She is struggling in her marriage, trying hard to keep her full-time job, and is constantly feeling the stress of life weigh her down. When Mary Jane was asked—what are your best qualities?—she gave a blank stare. She was blind to her signature strengths. She took the VIA Survey and discovered her signature strengths were fairness, curiosity, kindnes, and judgment/critical thinking. In many ways this was a re-discovery for Mary Jane. She had once known she had these wonderful qualities but over time life simply "got in the way" and her character strengths eroded – she forgot about them and hence forgot to use them in her life. By the time her children came along her personal strengths were far from her mind. The good news, which Mary Jane quickly realized, was that she could tap back into these strengths right away. Her strengths began to soar and her confidence as a parent re-emerged.

Which of the 24 strengths are your "signature"? To be sure, go to www.viame.org and take the self-assessment survey called the VIA Survey (VIA Inventory of Strengths). It is a free, valid, online test that will help you discover your highest strengths.

Write down five or six of your signature strengths:

_____

_____

_____

_____

_____

PHASE 2: EXPLORE

This phase involves digging in and investigating how and when you express your strengths. It involves considering when you've used the strength in the past, what strengths you tend to use in various situations of your present lifestyle, and how you might use your strengths more in the future.

You, an Excellent Parent

Think of a time when you did an excellent job parenting. Tell the story of a particular instance. Describe it in detail; explain the actions you took. Then, consider this: What were the character strengths you used in that positive experience?

_____

_____

_____

_____

Digging Deeper:

Here's another exercise for exploring your best qualities. Choose 1 of your signature strengths. Explore each of the following with that strength:

What does this character strength look like?

When and where can you use this strength in your daily life?

What do your family members and friends say when you use this strength?

What happens if you express too little of this strength? When does that usually occur?

What happens if you express too much of this strength? When does that usually occur?

What benefits does this strength bring to you and others?

_____

_____

_____

_____

_____

PHASE 3: APPLY

This phase involves making strengths part of your life routine. After reflecting upon, exploring, and discussing your strengths, it's time to impact your behavior.

Strengths, in a New Way

Research has found that individuals who use one of their signature strengths in a new way each day experience a number of benefits, such as an increase in happiness and a decrease in depression.

Choose one of your signature strengths. Use it in a new way each day. Find different ways to express the character strength each day. For example, if you choose curiosity, take a different route home and explore a new area or neighborhood. If you choose perseverance, complete a small project that you have been putting off. Stick with the practice for a couple weeks.

Set a Parenting Goal

After building your self-knowledge and exploring your strengths, you're ready to set a goal. You might consider setting a strengths-oriented goal related to good parenting. Consider:

- How might one of your signature strengths help you as a parent?

- Which of your signature strengths would bring the most benefit to your child?

- What might you do to use one of your signature strengths a little bit more in your parenting?

DR. MARGERY GINSBERG, director of the Leadership for Learning Program at the University of Washington, has created a simple survey that can help you get a sense of how supportive you child's school is to their motivation to learn and how supportive the school is to your interest in being involved in the school and your child's classroom. It will help quantify how you perceive that school personnel cares about you and your child.

If most of your answers are "Don't know," this is an indicator that you might want to consider getting more involved with your child's education and school. Next step, make an appointment with your child's teacher. And a good place to begin might be to bring along a copy of the Washington Student Success Promise. See Chapter 11

If most of your answers are a 1 or a 2, then you need to consider taking action to change the culture of your school. Next steps, confer with other parents. Ask them to take the survey. If their results are similar to yours, then it's time to set a meeting with the principal. Take a look at Chapters 11, 12 and 13 for some ideas on how to hold a constructive meeting with your school principal.

If most of your answers are a 4 or a 5, consider yourself fortunate. Your school appears to be responsive to you and your child's needs. Compare notes with other parents, if they agree, you may want to acknowledge and appreciate the school's teachers and leadership for creating this kind of learning community. It's a model we want as many schools as possible to adopt.

—Marc Sachnoff, Chief Parent, The Parents Union

DOES YOUR SCHOOL MOTIVATE YOUR CHILD?

PARENT SURVEY

(from *Motivation Matters*, by Margery Ginsberg, p. 120)

The Parent Survey elicits the parents or a custodial family member's perspective on the extent to which a school supports (1) their child's motivation to learn and (2) their family's motivation to be involved with their child's school. It aligns with "The Motivational Framework for Culturally Responsive Teaching," because both student and family motivation are essential to a student's emotional, social, and academic success in school. Parents can use the survey to think about how to advocate for their child's needs and their family's needs as members of the school community.

INSTRUCTIONS: Rate your agreement or disagreement with the statements below by circling a number from 1 to 5 (1 = strongly disagree; 5 = strongly agree) or circling Don't know."

INCLUSION

Information is communicated frequently and well.	1	2	3	4	5	Don't know
My child is treated fairly at school.	1	2	3	4	5	Don't know
I feel my child is safe in school.	1	2	3	4	5	Don't know
I feel that my child and I are welcome in school.	1	2	3	4	5	Don't know

The school is responsive to students' needs and interests.	1	2	3	4	5	Don't know
Leadership in this school is visible and strong.	1	2	3	4	5	Don't know
Parents are involved in making decisions in this school.	1	2	3	4	5	Don't know

ATTITUDE

The principal is interested in my concerns and problems.	1	2	3	4	5	Don't know
School staff members are available for conferences, and I have opportunities to voice my concerns.	1	2	3	4	5	Don't know
Teachers in this school seem to like being here.	1	2	3	4	5	Don't know
My child shows a feeling of excitement about going to school.	1	2	3	4	5	Don't know
I am satisfied with the level of homework required of my child.	1	2	3	4	5	Don't know
People I know speak favorably about this school.	1	2	3	4	5	Don't know

MEANING

I am given opportunities to be involved in my child's education in ways that I enjoy.	1	2	3	4	5	Don't know
My child seems bored at school.	1	2	3	4	5	Don't know
This school has high expectations for all students.	1	2	3	4	5	Don't know
I am enriched by my experiences with the school.	1	2	3	4	5	Don't know

COMPETENCE						
Teacher expectations are clear and understandable to my child.	1	2	3	4	5	Don't know
I am frequently informed about my child's progress.	1	2	3	4	5	Don't know
I am happy with my child's progress in school.	1	2	3	4	5	Don't know
This school places a high value on student success and achievement.	1	2	3	4	5	Don't know
My child feels successful at this school.	1	2	3	4	5	Don't know
I believe my participation at this school makes a big difference.	1	2	3	4	5	Don't know
This school helps me do a better job supporting my child's education.	1	2	3	4	5	Don't know

3

ABOUT MY CHILD

The Parental Journey Continues

Harvard Professor **HOWARD GARDNER** first proposed a theory of multiple intelligences in 1983. His work has been widely embraced (as well as challenged) because he theorized that what we consider intelligence might actually be eight very specific and primarily sensory ways that humans interact and process stimulus and information. Until Dr. Gardener came on the scene, most academics and researchers thought that intelligence was a single general ability. But any parent who knows his or her children realizes that each child has different approaches to learning. Some kids can read quietly for hours and others can't sit still for a minute—they need to be up and jumping around. One child may be able to memorize complex poems in rhyme while another finds calculating fractions in his or her head easy. Why is this possible if all intelligence is the same?

As you can imagine, Dr. Gardener's multiple intelligences framework has been a huge help to parents in trying to understand how their kids tick and how to inspire them to grow and develop in a healthy manner. Many schools have embraced Dr. Gardener's framework as well—but not all, and not consistently. That's why it's crucial—yes, *crucial*—that you understand how each of your children learns. In other words, which of these eight ways of learning or processing information best describes your child?

Once you have your child take the simple test in the links provided below, you may discover some very useful information that can assist you and your child's teachers in helping him or her become more successful in school.

Let's face it, if your kid is in a school or classroom that's all about teachers lecturing for hours at a time and your kid's dominant intelligence is kinesthetic—meaning he functions best when on his feet prancing around—there's going to be a problem.

And one final thought. You might want to take the test yourself. I did and it sure helped me understand why my son and I were not on the same wavelength about a number of things. He and I just process information differently, so there was no sense trying to make him do it my way when he would flourish if I just helped him learn the way he naturally learned best.

—Marc Sachnoff, Chief Parent, The Parents Union

HOWARD GARDNER'S MULTIPLE INTELLIGENCES

(adapted from www.businessballs.com/howardgardnermultipleintelligences.htm)

The more detailed diagram below expands the detail for the original seven intelligences shown above, and also suggests ideas for applying the model and underpinning theories, so as to optimise learning and training, design accelerated learning methods, and to assess training and learning suitability and effectiveness.

	intelligence type	description	typical roles	related tasks, activities or tests	preferred learning style clues
1	Linguistic	words and language, written and spoken; retention, interpretation and explanation of ideas and information via language, understands relationship between communication and meaning	writers, lawyers, journalists, speakers, trainers, copy-writers, english teachers, poets, editors, linguists, translators, PR consultants, media consultants, TV and radio presenters, voice-over artistes	write a set of instructions; speak on a subject; edit a written piece or work; write a speech; commentate on an event; apply positive or negative 'spin' to a story	words and language
2	Logical-Mathematical	logical thinking, detecting patterns, scientific reasoning and deduction; analyse problems, perform mathematical calculations, understands relationship between cause and effect towards a tangible outcome or result	scientists, engineers, computer experts, accountants, statisticians, researchers, analysts, traders, bankers bookmakers, insurance brokers, negotiators, deal-makers, troubleshooters, directors	perform a mental arithmetic calculation; create a process to measure something difficult; analyse how a machine works; create a process; devise a strategy to achieve an aim; assess the value of a business or a proposition	numbers and logic

3	Musical	musical ability, awareness, appreciation and use of sound; recognition of tonal and rhythmic patterns, understands relationship between sound and feeling	musicians, singers, composers, DJ's, music producers, piano tuners, acoustic engineers, entertainers, party-planners, environment and noise advisors, voice coaches	perform a musical piece; sing a song; review a musical work; coach someone to play a musical instrument; specify mood music for telephone systems and receptions	music, sounds, rhythm
4	Bodily-Kinesthetic	body movement control, manual dexterity, physical agility and balance; eye and body coordination	dancers, demonstrators, actors, athletes, divers, sports-people, soldiers, fire-fighters, PTI's, performance artistes; ergonomists, osteopaths, fishermen, drivers, craftspeople; gardeners, chefs, acupuncturists, healers, adventurers	juggle; demonstrate a sports technique; flip a beer-mat; create a mime to explain something; toss a pancake; fly a kite; coach workplace posture, assess work-station ergonomics	physical experience and movement, touch and feel
5	Spatial-Visual	visual and spatial perception; interpretation and creation of visual images; pictorial imagination and expression; understands relationship between images and meanings, and between space and effect	artists, designers, cartoonists, story-boarders, architects, photographers, sculptors, town-planners, visionaries, inventors, engineers, cosmetics and beauty consultants	design a costume; interpret a painting; create a room layout; create a corporate logo; design a building; pack a suitcase or the boot of a car	pictures, shapes, images, 3D space
6	Interpersonal	perception of other people's feelings; ability to relate to others; interpretation of behaviour and communications; understands the relationships between people and their situations, including other people	therapists, HR professionals, mediators, leaders, counsellors, politicians, eductors, sales-people, clergy, psychologists, teachers, doctors, healers, organisers, carers, advertising professionals, coaches and mentors; (there is clear association between this type of intelligence and what is now termed 'Emotional Intelligence' or EQ)	interpret moods from facial expressions; demonstrate feelings through body language; affect the feelings of others in a planned way; coach or counsel another person	human contact, communications, cooperation, teamwork

| 7 | Intrapersonal | self-awareness, personal cognisance, personal objectivity, the capability to understand oneself, one's relationship to others and the world, and one's own need for, and reaction to change | arguably anyone (see note below) who is self-aware and involved in the process of changing personal thoughts, beliefs and behaviour in relation to their situation, other people, their purpose and aims - in this respect there is a similarity to Maslow's Self-Actualization level, and again there is clear association between this type of intelligence and what is now termed 'Emotional Intelligence' or EQ | consider and decide one's own aims and personal changes required to achieve them (not necessarily reveal this to others); consider one's own 'Johari Window', and decide options for development; consider and decide one's own position in relation to the Emotional Intelligence model | self-reflection, self-discovery |

Roles and intrapersonal intelligence: Given that a "role" tends to imply external style/skills, engagement, etc., the intrapersonal ability is less liable to define or suggest a certain role or range of roles than any of the other characteristics. That said, there is a clear correlation between intrapersonal ability/potential and introverted non-judgmental roles/working styles. Intrapersonal capability might also be seen as the opposite of ego and self-projection. Self-awareness is a prerequisite for self-discipline and self-improvement. Intrapersonal capacity enables an emotionally mature ("grown-up") response to external and internal stimuli. The intrapersonal characteristic might therefore be found among (but most definitely not extending to all) counselors, helpers, translators, teachers, actors, poets, writers, musicians, artists, and also any other role to which people can bring emotional maturity, which commonly manifests as adaptability, flexibility, facilitation, reflection, and other 'grown-up' behaviours. There are also associations between intrapersonal capacity and Erikson's "generative" perspective, and to an extent <u>Maslow's</u> self-actualization, that is to say: both of these life-stages surely demand a reasonably strong level of self-awareness, without which adapting one's personal life, outlook and responses to one's environment is not easy at all.

Resources

- Businessballs.com: http://www.businessballs.com/howardgardnermultiple intelligences.htm#multiple%20intelligences%20tests

- Video of Howard Gardner: http://www.youtube.com/watch?v=I2QtSbP4FRg

- Teacher Education website: http://educ-reality.com/howard-gardners-multiple-intelligences/

- Linda Campbell, Bruce Campbell, Dee Dickinson, *Teaching and Learning through Multiple Intelligences* (Boston: Pearce Education, 2004)

RESOURCES

FROM RYAN NIEMIEC, VIA INSTITUTE

WEBSITE RESOURCES

Website: www.viame.org

Take the free online survey of character strengths. Adults take the VIA Inventory of Strengths (also called the VIA Survey) and youth from 10-17 take one of the youth surveys. Adults and youth receive immediate, free results – a rank-order of your 24 character strengths with brief descriptions of each. Adults and youth have the option to pay for more in-depth reports that include a deep, personal analysis of your strengths, several graphs, and other user-friendly material. [Editor's Note: The Parents Union derives no financial benefit from these tests.]

- *VIA Me Pathways Report*: A consumer-friendly report with graphs, tips, quotes, and strategies for working with one's highest character strengths.

- *VIA Pro Report*: An extensive report used to help practitioners better understand their client's strengths; reviews signature strengths, the latest research, & best practices.

- *VIA Pro TEAM Report*: An extensive report designed for consultants and leaders in the business world to capitalize and leverage team strengths.

Website: www.viapros.org

In addition to being a parent, if you are also a teacher, educator, consultant, coach, counselor, manager/business-professional working with a team of employees, or another type of practitioner, then this is the right website for you! This website is stocked full of free resources that includes stories, leading practitioners sharing their strength practices, movie examples, inspiring videos, and user-friendly research summaries. There are also online courses and workshops practitioners can take to learn all they'd ever want to know about applying character strengths to help individuals and groups.

BOOK RESOURCES

- *Authentic Happiness* (2002) by Martin Seligman. This book is a good introduction to positive psychology and character strengths.

- *Celebrating Strengths* (2008) by Jenny Fox Eades. This book is for teachers and school professionals interested in bringing character strengths into the school culture.

- *Positive Psychology at the Movies* by Ryan M. Niemiec and Danny Wedding. This book reviews each of the 24 character strengths and the best movies that portray them. Useful for practical exercises involving "strengths heroes."

- *Smart Strengths* (2011) by John Yeager, Sherri Fisher, and David Shearon. This guide-book is for parents, teachers, and coaches interested in building character strengths and resilience in youth.

- *Strengths Gym* (2011) by Carmel Proctor and Jenny Fox Eades. This practical book focuses on various exercises for working with each of the 24 character strengths. It comes with a CD of worksheets and exercises.

4

WHAT IS 21ST CENTURY PARENTING?

Dealing with behavior issues is a constant problem for many parents. Whether you're at home with a sibling explosion in front of the TV or at a restaurant with a child who has decided to order three types of dessert for his or her lunch, we've all been in a situation where we wished we had some good advice on how to transform a bad scene into a good one. Thankfully, our friend, **JOE NEWMAN** has worked with some of the most difficult kids you can imagine—and helped them find a way to express their energy and passion constructively. Joe's piece helps parents create clear, loving and consistent boundaries that can help children develop healthy independence. It's not easy, but if you apply these ideas consistently along with your spouse, partner and other caregivers, you can make amazing progress.

—Marc Sachnoff, Chief Parent, The Parents Union

FEEDING CANDY TO LIONS

(from *Raising Lions*, by Joe Newman, www.raisinglions.com)

While there is a degree of empowering choices that's healthy to give a child, this is a fundamental shift from thirty or forty years ago, and it's changing the way our children view themselves. When children get used to having choices about everything, they come to expect to be given choices about everything. By the time they enter school, many children aren't ready for a teacher who doesn't ask them, but tells them what activity will come next.

Instead of this	Try this
Giving choices about everything. Clothes, food, activities, schedule, etc…. "Where would you like to go to eat?" "What time do you want to go to the park?"	**Choices about some things and not others.** "Mommy and Daddy choose where we're going to eat. At the restaurant you'll have some choices about what you'll order." "We're going to the park at 1:00." "When we go to the park you must always wear pants."
Open-ended choices "What do you want to wear today?" "What do you want to order?"	**Structured choices** "Which pants would you like to wear? The red or the blue?" "You can order the macaroni, the fish, or the hot dog."
There are always choices	**Sometimes the only choice is between doing what Mommy says or getting a consequence.**
Allowing long discussion or debate about the choices and the rules "But I don't want to go home. I want to stay at the park."	**There should be times when "no discussion" is the rule.** While short discussions should sometimes be accommodated, if your child is using questioning the rule as a way to badger you into relenting, you should give a consequence that deters them from using this approach again: "I told you I wasn't going to discuss this any more, now you'll need to take a two-minute time out."
Having choices is a right	**Having choices is a privilege that can be taken away if you don't respect the rules that govern them.**

Using the options above will allow you to create a structure within which to manage your child's wants and desires. Only after the parent has created such a structure can the child begin to internalize that structure and develop the muscles needed for self-regulation and deferred gratification.

TIPS FOR PARENTS

Instead of this	Try this
Asking them to apologize. "Tell your sister you're sorry." "I need you to apologize to Kevin and tell him you won't hit him again."	Give an immediate consequence. The consequence needs to be sufficient to outweigh the gain from the problem behavior. In other words you want them to feel sorry they did the behavior, not just say it.
Telling them how they should feel. "Look at your sister crying. Don't you feel sad for her?"	Let consequences teach. When adults try to tell children what they should feel (empathy, compassion, generosity, etc.) what they actually feel is shame and guilt because they didn't have those feelings.
Explaining to them in detail why something is wrong.	Ask them to figure it out. After giving a consequence, ask them questions so they can see the behavior wasn't in their self-interest. "Why did you…" "Did that choice get you what you wanted?" "What could you have done to get what you wanted?"
Repeatedly telling your son and his friend to stop yelling while they are watching TV.	Take the remote and turn the TV off. Now that you have their attention, tell them: "The TV is turned off for the next minute. If I have to do this again it will be turned off for five minutes. Do you understand why I turned it off?"
Telling them the rules over and over. When you tell children the rules over and over again you are trying to protect them from failure, mistakes and consequences. By letting them learn from consequences you allow them how to relax and evolve through their mistakes.	**Tell them the rule once, or not at all.** After that give short consequences so they remember and learn the rules. Repeating the rules over and over is condescending and tells them the rules aren't serious. Violent or destructive acts should be met with immediate consequences. If your four-year-old daughter throws her plate, there is no need to explain why that's not OK.

CHARACTERISTICS OF THE OMNIPOTENT IDENTITY CHILD

(Editor's Note: Mr. Newman describes the development of the child's self-identity, the second stage of which is omnipotence: "Anxiety and fear from the toddler's newly realized vulnerability drive the child to try and make his world safer by attempting to assert his will over everything…. The child becomes a tyrant in an attempt to get the parents to give him not only everything he needs, but everything he *wants*…. Because the child has now shifted into imposing his newly discovered willpower over others, but hasn't yet discovered that others have wants, needs and willpower of their own, this second stage is called **omnipotence**." He refers to the child in this stage as an O.I. [omnipotent identity] child.)

While the O.I. child continues to develop in other areas, his self-identity and the emotional framework from which he views himself and others remains stuck in the omnipotent stage. His tantrums and manipulations become stronger and more complex as he gets older and makes use of more highly developed communication, physical, and cognitive skills. Omnipotence in children can manifest as several or all of the following six characteristics.

1. **Manipulative**: Emma's feeling that she was more powerful than anyone else, and therefore the person most in control, fueled her anxiety that the world around her was unsafe and that she needed to control it. With each successful power struggle, tantrum or manipulation, Emma's manipulative skills became stronger and more complex. She engaged in manipulation compulsively because it brought her comfort knowing she could control things. However, with each successful manipulation, whether it was convincing her counselor she was too upset to do math or creating so much tension that her teacher ignored her rather than insist she

work with the rest of the class, Emma's sense of her own omnipotence increased—and with it, her anxiety of living in a world where she alone was in control.

2. **Oppositional and defiant**: Emma does not recognize others as equals. Like the Kevin McAllister character in *Home Alone*, she is more competent than all others. Because she has not transitioned to recognizing others as independent and with their own power, her emotional instincts perceive others as either unruly extensions of herself or simply as obstacles to her omnipotent will. She is caught in an emotional catch-22. Because she feels omnipotent, she is alone in the world and responsible for keeping things in control. Her opposition and defiance are another expression of the tantruming child whose hand pushes forward and says, "I'm here and I have power. Does anyone else have power like me?" She is still trying to gain the recognition that can only be given by someone who has been established as equal to or stronger than she is.

3. **Emotionally volatile**: The O.I. child has an underdeveloped capacity to process frustration and disappointment and can be quick to break down in tears or fly into a rage. This is due to three factors. First, the O.I. child has placed unreasonable pressure on herself to control everything. Second, children like Emma never made enough of a shift from demanding that things outside of them change (externalizing) to adjusting themselves to deal with frustration or disappointment (internalizing). Because she succeeded in continuing to externalize emotional difficulties, Emma consequently underdeveloped the emotional muscles needed to process difficulties and frustrations. Lastly, emotional

outbursts may have been reinforced because they were an effective way to manipulate adults and get them to capitulate to her wishes. In other words, Emma's emotional volatility became an effective tool for exerting control.

4. **Inability to accept correction, consequence or direction** and/or the need to always be part of every decision: One of the consequences of the current child rearing practice of giving a child a choice about everything is that it reinforces the misconception that children should have control over any decision made that affects them. Consequently, they feel entitled to argue every decision they don't prefer until they are either convinced of the direction or they have convinced the adult to change the decision to accord with their preference. Why should a child who feels omnipotent take correction, consequence, or direction from an adult she perceives as her lesser?

5. **An obsession with everything being fair**: One of the difficulties the school staff had with Emma was her constant complaint that things weren't fair. "That's not fair! Hannah was fooling around too! Why do I have to stay in for recess?" "That's not fair, why does Zach get to erase the board! He did it yesterday!" The "it's not fair" argument was both a compulsive response to anything Emma didn't like and a manipulation to get what she wanted. She was so astute at finding flaws and inconsistencies in those around her that when we started using a behavior plan at school she would complain to her mother any time a staff member didn't follow the script exactly. "I wouldn't have gotten so upset if Felicia

hadn't said she was sick of me. You shouldn't be able to say that to kids. She should be fired." I would get calls from her mother relaying exaggerated tales of what the staff said or did that wasn't perfect and were the cause of Emma's outbursts. This behavior is a consequence of allowing a child to continue to externalize problems and frustrations. The once healthy tendency of the infant to look to the caregiver (seen as an extension of them) to meet all her needs and resolve her frustrations (make everything fair) grows into an inability to accept any disappointment or difficulty. If Emma felt frustrated or unsatisfied with a situation or outcome, she assumed that the source of the problem was external and unjust (unfair) and should be changed to relieve her discomfort.

6. **Perfectionist tendencies**: Emma needed to be the best speller in the class in order to feel secure because of her belief that everything was up to her to control. She placed enormous pressure on herself to do things perfectly. This was fueled by the anxiety that comes from feeling that if she didn't control things they would be out of control. Because she won the majority of power struggles with her caregivers, she perceived herself as not only most powerful, but also the most responsible for keeping things safe.

THE MYTH OF NOT KNOWING

There is a myth that if children aren't behaving appropriately it's because they don't know how to behave appropriately. As a result, when children misbehave adults explain things that children already know. But explaining something to a child that he already knows, or speaking in a manner that infers as much, will develop a dysfunctional communication dynamic, feed omnipotence and breed manipulation.

When I started to work with children, I often saw this dynamic between teachers and students in the classroom and between parents and children in the home. Adults were constantly telling children rules and boundaries they already knew. Over the course of some years I was able to break down this dynamic so as to better understand it, reverse it and create motivating interactions.

If you listen to what's said in a classroom or at home, you can divide the inappropriate behaviors into three types, and the responses to those behaviors into five types. The three types of behavior are benign, malignant and impulsive.

Benign behavior—Five-year-old Mia leaves kindergarten class to go to the bathroom without asking or telling anyone because she didn't know the rules. Benign behavior occurs because the child doesn't understand the behavior is not acceptable (positive intention).

Malignant behavior—Eight-year-old Tony throws a paper airplane at another student while the teacher's back is turned. Malignant behavior is behavior that the child understands, or could reasonably figure out, is not acceptable (negative intention).

Impulsive behavior—A student calls out the answer to the teacher's question without raising his hand because he is excited that he knows the answer. Impulsive behavior occurs as a reaction to something or as an impulse without any time to think. The child understands the behavior is unacceptable but acts before thinking (no intention). There are five types of responses to problem behaviors: Information, Action, Ignore/Accommodate, Question and Inappropriate.

Information response—The teacher says to Mia, "Leaving class without permission is not allowed. If you need to leave the class, then ask me so I know where you are." An information response is a response that gives information. (Give information.)

Action response—After he throws the plane, Tony is told he needs to move to a desk in front next to the teacher. This is a response that requires an immediate action or delivers an immediate consequence. (Give a consequence.)

Ignore/Accommodate response—"The teacher can see by the look on William's face that he realized he should have raised his hand before calling out, so she ignores his outburst and continues her teaching. Some behaviors are minor enough to ignore, and others, like squirming around in your seat or needing to stand or pace, can be accommodated so they are not disruptive. (Allow the behavior.)

Question response—Dana is talking to Abigail while her teacher is trying to lead a lesson so her teacher says to Dana, "Dana, do you need to move to another seat?" (Ask the student to make a choice.)

Inappropriate response—"I'm sick of telling you to shut your mouth when I'm teaching." There are an infinite variety of inappropriate responses to children including yelling, insulting, sarcasm, threats and rhetorical questions. All of these build a pattern of disrespect and should never be used.

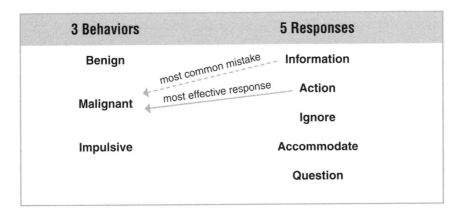

3 Behaviors	5 Responses
Benign	Information
Malignant	Action
	Ignore
Impulsive	Accommodate
	Question

most common mistake
most effective response

Each of the three behaviors above has responses that build healthy communication with children and responses that undermine them.

I love education gadfly **ALFIE KOHN**, not just because I always agree with him, but because he makes me reconsider my attitudes and underlying beliefs—and that's a good thing. But rather than say "Good job, Alfie!" I have to consider the mixed messages inherent in the kind of automatic praise I have been giving my kids—and the grownups in my life, too. For a short clip of Alfie on this, see http://youtu.be/QQesSzkZW4s]http://youtu.be/QQesSzkZW4s.

From Alfie's piece, we learn that saying "Good job!" can undermine independence, pleasure, interest, and also interfere with, as Alfie writes, "how good a job children actually do." I firmly believe that human beings benefit from the sincere recognition of their efforts by others. And while Alfie insists he's not suggesting that kids don't need love and support from us, he makes some thought-provoking points on the kind of automatic praise many of us do all the time that are worth considering.

—Marc Sachnoff, Chief Parent, The Parents Union

FIVE REASONS TO STOP SAYING "GOOD JOB!"

BY ALFIE KOHN

Hang out at a playground, visit a school, or show up at a child's birthday party, and there's one phrase you can count on hearing repeatedly: "Good job!" Even tiny infants are praised for smacking their hands together ("Good clapping!"). Many of us blurt out these judgments of our children to the point that it has become almost a verbal tic.

Plenty of books and articles advise us against relying on punishment, from spanking to forcible isolation ("time out"). Occasionally someone will even ask us to rethink the practice of bribing children with stickers or food. But you'll have to look awfully hard to find a discouraging word about what is euphemistically called positive reinforcement.

Lest there be any misunderstanding, the point here is not to call into question the importance of supporting and encouraging children, the need to love them and hug them and help them feel good about themselves. Praise, however, is a different story entirely. Here's why.

1. **Manipulating children**. Suppose you offer a verbal reward to reinforce the behavior of a two-year-old who eats without spilling, or a five-year-old who cleans up her art supplies. Who benefits from this? Is it possible that telling kids they've done a good job may have less to do with their emotional needs than with our convenience?

Rheta DeVries, a professor of education at the University of Northern Iowa, refers to this as "sugar-coated control." Very much like tangible rewards—or, for that matter, punishments—it's a way of doing something *to* children to get them to comply with our wishes. It may be effective at producing this result (at least for a while), but it's very different from working *with* kids—for example, by engaging them in conversation about what makes a classroom (or family) function smoothly, or how other people are affected by what we have done—or failed to do. The latter approach is not only more respectful but more likely to help kids become thoughtful people.

The reason praise can work in the short run is that young children are hungry for our approval. But we have a responsibility not to exploit that dependence for our own convenience. A "Good job!" to reinforce something that makes our lives a little easier can be an example of taking advantage of children's dependence. Kids may also come to feel manipulated by this, even if they can't quite explain why.

2. **Creating praise junkies**. To be sure, not every use of praise is a calculated tactic to control children's behavior. Sometimes we compliment kids just because we're genuinely pleased by what they've done. Even then, however, it's worth looking more closely. Rather than bolstering a child's self-esteem, praise may increase kids' dependence on us. The more we say, "I like the way you…" or "Good _____ing," the more kids come to rely on *our* evaluations, *our* decisions about what's good and bad, rather than learning to form their own judgments. It leads them to measure their worth in terms of what will lead *us* to smile and dole out some more approval.

Mary Budd Rowe, a researcher at the University of Florida, discovered that students who were praised lavishly by their teachers were more tentative in their responses, more apt to answer in a questioning tone of voice ("Um, seven?"). They tended to back off from an idea they had proposed as soon as an adult disagreed with them. And they were less likely to persist with difficult tasks or share their ideas with other students.

In short, "Good job!" doesn't reassure children; ultimately, it makes them feel less secure. It may even create a vicious circle such that the more we slather on the praise, the more kids seem to need it, so we praise them some more. Sadly, some of these kids will grow into adults who continue to need someone else to pat them on the head and tell them whether what they did was OK. Surely this is not what we want for our daughters and sons.

3. **Stealing a child's pleasure**. Apart from the issue of dependence, a child deserves to take delight in her accomplishments, to feel pride in what she's learned how to do. She also deserves to decide when to feel that way. Every time we say, "Good job!", though, we're telling a child how to feel.

To be sure, there are times when our evaluations are appropriate and our guidance is necessary—especially with toddlers and preschoolers. But a constant stream of value judgments is neither necessary nor useful for children's development. Unfortunately, we may not have realized that "Good job!" is just as much an evaluation as "Bad job!" The most notable feature of a positive judgment isn't that it's positive, but that it's a judgment. And people, including kids, don't like being judged.

I cherish the occasions when my daughter manages to do something for the first time, or does something better than she's ever done it before. But I try to resist the knee-jerk tendency to say, "Good job!" because I don't want to dilute her joy. I want her to share her pleasure with me, not look to me for a verdict. I want her to exclaim, "I did it!" (which she often does) instead of asking me uncertainly, "Was that good?"

4. **Losing interest**. "Good painting!" may get children to keep painting for as long as we keep watching and praising. But, warns Lilian Katz, one of the country's leading authorities on early childhood education, "once attention is withdrawn, many kids won't touch the activity again." Indeed, an impressive body of scientific research has shown that the more we reward people for doing something, the more they tend to lose interest in whatever they had to do to get the reward. Now the point isn't to draw, to read, to think, to create—the point is to get the goody, whether it's an ice cream, a sticker, or a "Good job!"

In a troubling study conducted by Joan Grusec at the University of Toronto, young children who were frequently praised for displays of generosity tended to be slightly *less* generous on an everyday basis than other children were. Every time they had heard "Good sharing!" or "I'm so proud of you for helping," they became a little less interested in sharing or helping. Those actions came to be seen not as something valuable in their own right but as something they had to do to get that reaction again from an adult. Generosity became a means to an end.

Does praise motivate kids? Sure. It motivates kids to get praise. Alas, that's often at the expense of commitment to whatever they were doing that prompted the praise.

5. **Reducing achievement**. As if it weren't bad enough that "Good job!" can undermine independence, pleasure, and interest, it can also interfere with how good a job children actually do. Researchers keep finding that kids who are praised for doing well at a creative task tend to stumble at the next task—and they don't do as well as children who weren't praised to begin with.

Why does this happen? Partly because the praise creates pressure to "keep up the good work" that gets in the way of doing so. Partly because their *interest* in what they're doing may have declined. Partly because they become less likely to take risks—a prerequisite for creativity—once they start thinking about how to keep those positive comments coming.

More generally, "Good job!" is a remnant of an approach to psychology that reduces all of human life to behaviors that can be seen and measured. Unfortunately, this ignores the thoughts, feelings, and values that lie behind behaviors. For example, a child may share a snack with a friend as a way of attracting praise, or as a way of making sure the other child has enough to eat. Praise for sharing ignores these different motives. Worse, it actually promotes the less desirable motive by making children more likely to fish for praise in the future.

■　■　■

Once you start to see praise for what it is—and what it does—these constant little evaluative eruptions from adults start to produce the same effect as fingernails being dragged down a blackboard. You begin to root for a child to give his teachers or parents a taste of their own treacle by turning around to them and saying (in the same saccharine tone of voice), "Good praising!"

Still, it's not an easy habit to break. It can seem strange, at least at first, to stop praising; it can feel as though you're being chilly or withholding something. But that, it soon becomes clear, suggests that *we praise more because we need to say it than because children need to hear it.* Whenever that's true, it's time to rethink what we're doing.

What kids do need is unconditional support, love with no strings attached. That's not just different from praise—it's the *opposite* of praise. "Good job!" is conditional. It means we're offering attention and acknowledgement and approval for jumping through our hoops, for doing things that please us.

This point, you'll notice, is very different from a criticism that some people offer to the effect that we give kids too much approval, or give it too easily. They recommend that we become more miserly with our praise and demand that kids "earn" it. But the real problem isn't that children expect to be praised for everything they do these days. It's that *we're* tempted to take shortcuts, to manipulate kids with rewards instead of explaining and helping them to develop needed skills and good values.

So what's the alternative? That depends on the situation, but whatever we decide to say instead has to be offered in the context of genuine affection and love for who kids are rather than for what they've done. When unconditional support is present, "Good job!" isn't necessary; when it's absent, "Good job!" won't help.

If we're praising positive actions as a way of discouraging misbehavior, this is unlikely to be effective for long. Even when it works, we can't really say the child is now "behaving himself"; it would be more accurate to say the praise is behaving him. The alternative is to work *with* the child, to figure out the reasons he's acting that way. We may have to reconsider our own requests rather than just looking for a way to get kids to obey. (Instead of using "Good job!" to get a four-year-old to sit quietly through a long class meeting or family dinner, perhaps we should ask whether it's reasonable to expect a child to do so.)

We also need to bring kids in on the process of making decisions. If a child is doing something that disturbs others, then sitting down with her later and asking, "What do you think we can do to solve this problem?" will likely be more effective than bribes or threats. It also helps a child learn how to solve problems and teaches that her ideas and feelings are important. Of course, this process takes time and talent, care and courage. Tossing off a "Good job!" when the child acts in the way we deem appropriate takes none of those things, which helps to explain why "doing to" strategies are a lot more popular than "working with" strategies.

And what can we say when kids just do something impressive? Consider three possible responses:

- **Say nothing.** Some people insist a helpful act must be "reinforced" because, secretly or unconsciously, they believe it was a fluke. If children are basically evil, then they have to be given an artificial reason for being nice (namely, to get a verbal reward). But if that cynicism is unfounded—and a lot of research suggests that it is—then praise may not be necessary.

- **Say what you saw.** A simple, evaluation-free statement ("You put your shoes on by yourself" or even just "You did it") tells your child that you noticed. It also lets her take pride in what she did. In other cases, a more elaborate description may make sense. If your child draws a picture, you might provide feedback—not judgment—

about what you noticed: "This mountain is huge!" "Boy, you sure used a lot of purple today!"

If a child does something caring or generous, you might gently draw his attention to the effect of his action *on the other person*: "Look at Abigail's face! She seems pretty happy now that you gave her some of your snack." This is completely different from praise, where the emphasis is on how *you* feel about her sharing

- **Talk less, ask more.** Even better than descriptions are questions. Why tell him what part of his drawing impressed you when you can ask him what he likes best about it? Asking "What was the hardest part to draw?" or "How did you figure out how to make the feet the right size?" is likely to nourish his interest in drawing. Saying "Good job!", as we've seen, may have exactly the opposite effect.

This doesn't mean that all compliments, all thank-you's, all expressions of delight are harmful. We need to consider our *motives* for what we say (a genuine expression of enthusiasm is better than a desire to manipulate the child's future behavior) as well as the actual *effects* of doing so. Are our reactions helping the child to feel a sense of control over her life—or to constantly look to us for approval? Are they helping her to become more excited about what she's doing in its own right—or turning it into something she just wants to get through in order to receive a pat on the head

It's not a matter of memorizing a new script, but of keeping in mind our long-term goals for our children and watching for the effects of what we say. The bad news is that the use of positive reinforcement really isn't so positive. The good news is that you don't have to evaluate in order to encourage.

NOTE: An abridged version of this article was published in Parents maga-zine in May 2000 with the title "Hooked on Praise." For a more detailed look at the issues discussed here—as well as a comprehensive list of citations to relevant research—please see the books Punished by Rewards and Unconditional Parenting. *(Para leer este artículo en Español, haga clic aquí.)*

Healthy Attachment is a healthy emotional state that parents can help babies achieve that can set the stage for positive development throughout the child's life. In the following two articles, psychologist **YAFFA MARITZ** lays out the characteristics of Healthy Attachment.

—Marc Sachnoff, Chief Parent, The Parents Union

ATTACHMENT PARENTING; WHAT'S IT ALL ABOUT?

BY YAFFA MARITZ

A cross the ocean in the United Kingdom in about 1950 when John Bowlby, a well-known psychologist and researcher, said to parents in his famous speech: "All of us find security in being with people we know well and are apt to feel anxious and insecure in crowds of strangers. Particularly in times of crisis or distress do we seek our closest friends. the need for companionship and the comfort it brings is a very deep need in human nature… and it is even stronger in infants."

Much of the subsequent research in child development confirmed that a child who forms healthy attachment to his primary care taker, will establish a "secure base." Having secure base will allow the child to accomplish the important tasks of the first years of life: developing warm, loving, trust worthy relationships (bids for closeness and intimacy) and exploring the world around him (seeds of autonomy and independence). We also know with the rising amount on brain research that the quality of attachment impacts the baby's social emotional and intellectual development.

The baby's feeling of trust develops at the same time that trillions of connections are forming in the language, intellectual, sensory and motor areas of the brain. The baby's experiences of love, trust, safety and exploration can become the permanent part of the brain structure. Moreover, the quality of interaction the baby has with his parents will lay the foundation for the creation internal "working models" of self and others. The more positive the experiences are, the more valuable and special the baby will feel he is, and the more trustworthy the baby will feel the people around him are.

So, what are the characteristics of healthy attachment? Daniel Siegel, a neuropsychologist from UCLA, wrote in his book *Parenting from the Inside Out* that the best predictor for healthy attachment is the ability of the parents to have a contingent communication with their child. Already in the early seventies, Mary Ainsworth, a psychologist and researcher from Johns Hopkins University saw the importance of Contingent Communication in establishing secure attachment, (although she did not use this term). In her research, contingent communication had 4 parts:

1. **Sensitivity to cues**
2. **Acceptance of the baby** as opposed to rejection
3. **Cooperation with the baby's rhythm**
4. **Emotional accessibility to the infant** (which includes having pleasure in their interaction)

Since securely attached children are generally happier, more curious, more self sufficient, better adjusted, more resilient to stress, handle conflict better, able to mange feelings better and are more successful socially and at school, it is our responsibility as a society to create climate that promotes healthy attachment.

We designed a program that does exactly that. The Listening Mothers program is helping mothers of infants to become more self-reflective and make better sense of their own life experiences.

In the supportive environment of the group, mothers share their stories as well explore the evolving relationship with their infants.

What a better gift can we give mothers, fathers and infants and all of us who surround them, than an opportunity to establish long lasting healthy relationships?

In May 2012, *Time* magazine ran a cover story titled "Are You Mom Enough?" It raised a lot of heated debate about parenting styles and Attachment Parenting in particular. At The Parents Union, our goal is to help all kids become happy, healthy, resilient, independent individuals who can maximize their unique potential and live meaningful and valuable lives. In psychologist **YAFFA MARITZ**'s piece, she wades into the turbulent waters surrounding the so-called Mommy Wars and finds that parenting is less about rigid approaches and more about raising successful kids.

—Marc Sachnoff, Chief Parent, The Parents Union

MOM'S HOT BUTTON

BY YAFFA MARITZ

The Community of Mindful Parents www.communityof mindfulparents.com got an urgent call from KIRO radio asking us to participate in an interview regarding the cover of the latest *Time* magazine article, titled "Are You Mom Enough?" (May 2012). The image went viral on the Internet before the actual magazine was out on the magazine shelves.

You can listen to the interview by clicking here: www.communityofmindfulparents.com/what-is-attachment-parenting-all-about-listen-to-bill-radke-treatment-podcast/.

The big question that this image elicits should not be around which side we take but rather what is it really that pushes our buttons? Why do new moms, who are mostly sensitive, dedicated, informed, and committed, get so easily triggered by purposefully provocative titles such as "Are You Mom Enough?" What is it that makes moms show their insecurities and confusion regarding what is best for their child?

Part of the answer lies in what we have written on our Community of Mindful Parents blog before; too much conflicting information and too little trust in one's own intuition and natural instincts. Yet the so-called Mommy Wars has its roots even deeper and broader than the individual psyche alone.

What seems to be at risk here and now gets questioned all the time is whether *motherhood* and modern *feminism* are mutually exclusive. (See, for example, the newly translated book by Elisabeth Badinter, "*The Conflict: How Modern Motherhood Undermined the Statue of Women.*")

What seems to be to lie at the heart of this question is a total misunderstanding of what Secure Attachment really is and what research tells us are those best child rearing practices that lead to the overall well-being of the child and the family.

Attachment Parenting, that style of parenting that originated by Dr. Sears and became popular after he published *The Baby Book* in 1992, is, as the article in the *Times* points out, "a style that is more about parental devotion and sacrifice than about raising self-sufficient kids," p. 34.

This is an important point. Moms in our society, in the US particularly, are presented with an impossible dilemma.

1. You work hard, living the feminist movement's dream, climb the cooperate ladder and be "successful." Or maybe you work because you have to for any number of reasons. However, as a society, since we do not provide moms with affordable child care, maternity leave, longer vacations, or flexible work hours we offer little to no support helping raise well adjusted children and many moms in this category end up exhausted and guilt ridden.

2. You stay home and adopt the "attachment parenting" style, which allows you to feel focused, dedicated, hard working, purposeful, and useful and feel like your long

years of being educated did not go to waist since you are "serving" your child. Moms in this category are often on the defensive as the "stay at home mom" has not been seen as a glamorous profession and their way to ward off criticism is to become more militant about their parenting philosophy (for reference, see the cover of Time Magazine photo of the Mom and 4 year old child breast feeding, which seemed to me more about defiance than about bonding and nurturing.)

[Of course, there are some moms who regardless of their philosophy are not presented with a choice as they need to support their family financially and are not always able to practice the ideal child rearing philosophy of their heart inclination.]

But have we thrown the baby out with the bath water, so to speak? So far, everywhere we read about the "mommy wars" we focus mostly on the parent needs and agenda and not so much on the child's needs. What does the child need to thrive?

In *Zero to Three*, a recent article titled "How Emotional Development Unfolds from Birth," Ross Thompson, a professor of psychology at the University of California Davis, emphasizes the importance of being attentive parents but at the same time allowing the child the opportunities to cope with frustrations and with not getting what they want whenever they want it. To quote, "More than ensuring that the child is happy all the time, an important goal for parents is helping to ensure that their child becomes competent, and competency arises from having to con-front things that frustrate her/him....The child needs to have the experience of developing the tools of self-control that sometimes develops when something they really want is not something they can have" (*Zero to Three*, January 2012, volume 32, p. 10).

A similar argument is brought up in Pamela Druckerman's book *Bringing Up BeBe*" (another one of those "in your face" but illuminating books, challenging the American moms, subtitled: "One American Mother Discovers the Wisdom of French Parenting"). In a chapter titled "Wait," Druckerman praises with amazement and amusement the benefits of the "pause." In her own words, "The French seem collectively to have achieved the miracle of getting babies and toddlers not just to wait, but to do so happily!" (p. 57), and she adds, "In the French view, having self-control to be calmly present, rather than…demanding, is what allows kids to have fun."

Secure Attachment is not about agenda-driven parenting. It is about being present in an attuned way to your child's needs, responding with wisdom and calm. Research in Secure Attachment shows that children who grow up in an environment where the parents are warm and loving, consistent and responsive, will grow up to have positive self-regard, resiliency, and competence. Parents who raise securely attached children realize that it is unrealistic to aspire to be "a perfect parent" or to always strive to fulfill all their kid's whims. How parents deal with ruptures, mistakes, frustrations, and limit setting are just as important building blocks for self-esteem, emotional security, and creativity as fun, playful times.

Whether you are a working mom, a stay-home mom, an attachment-parenting mom, or a French mom, please remember to treasure those moments of truly connecting with your child in a loving, warm way. The gift of a mom who is present lasts a lifetime. And wouldn't it be made so much easier if our society, here in our very own country, had our backs as well?

RESOURCES:

- The Community of Mindful Parents website, which includes a link to The Listening Mothers program: www.communityofmindfulparents.com

JULIE ROSS's *How to Hug a Porcupine* is an excellent book for parents who wake up one day to discover their cuddly, lovable kid has somehow become Godzilla overnight. In this piece Julie tackles the resentments, snarkyness, and lack of trust that can emanate from our teens and tweens and shares what she calls the "sandwich technique" —a way to work with our kids so that we can help insure their growing independence unfolds in a healthy and constructive way.

—Marc Sachnoff, Chief Parent, The Parents Union

HOW TO BREAK THE NAGGING CYCLE AND TURN RESPONSIBILITY OVER TO YOUR MIDDLE SCHOOLER

(from *How To Hug a Porcupine*, by Julie A. Ross, M.A., pp. 41–59)

Samantha, a bright, energetic mom in her early forties, looks dejected when she arrives at our parenting group. Her normal, upbeat energy is missing this morning, and she collapses into a chair. "I've had it," she says bleakly. "Honestly, I'm completely overwhelmed with Nick. I haven't felt this way since he was a toddler." The group looks at her expectantly. She shakes her head in disbelief. "I can't get him to brush his teeth in the morning. I know that sounds small, and stupid and crazy, but it's driving me nuts."

The group nods empathetically. They understand Samantha's exhaustion, because, while arguing with your child about brushing his teeth in the morning may be a "small" thing, it's not insignificant or uncommon.

Another mom, normally easygoing and calm, speaks up, her voice agitated: "Why do they do this? I don't understand it. I'm having a similar problem with Asanti. I ask her if she's done something—it could be anything: brushing her teeth, putting her homework in her bag, anything—and she scowls and gets this attitude and says, 'I can't believe you don't *trust* me,' and then she storms off. Of course, then I feel guilty for not trusting her, but you know what? She doesn't deserve my trust, because a lot of the time, she says she did something, but she really didn't! With that track record, why should I trust her?"

Why indeed? And why is it that elementary school children can go from willingly accepting instructions from Mom or Dad to brush their teeth, put on a jacket, shower, and all the other myriad things we ask them to do on a daily basis to being middle schoolers who resist (sometimes vehemently) these gentle reminders?

FEELINGS RUN DEEP

The answer is that middle schoolers feel things more deeply than ever before, and they often take our comments very personally. In a developmental period during which their very sense of who they are is rapidly changing, simple queries are heard as nagging. Gentle reminders are heard as insults. Thus, when Mom or Dad asks a simple question about teeth brushing or putting books in a bag, what the preteen hears is markedly different from what the parent actually says.

Let's take a look at some of the interpretations that preteens might make from a simple question by Mom or Dad:

What you say	What they hear
"Did you brush your teeth?"	"You can't look after yourself."
"Is your homework in your bag?"	"I don't trust you."
"Did you shower?"	"You look/smell bad."
"Have you finished your homework?"	"You're a poor student."

Clearly, when Asanti retaliated with "I can't believe you don't trust me," she was responding to what she thought she heard, not to what Mom actually said. And Nick, rather than talking back to his mother, chose to resist brushing his teeth in an effort to prove that he's independent.

"Well, what am I supposed to do?" Samantha asks. "Am I supposed to just let him go without brushing his teeth? Let him get the cavities? Will he learn then?"

NATURAL CONSEQUENCES

Samantha's question is a good one. Natural consequences—those things that happen as a direct result of our children's actions without parental interference—can be powerful teachers. Think about it: how many times does a toddler touch a hot stove? Only once, if at all. Why? The direct result of the action is uncomfortable, and the child learns quickly from discomfort.

Sometimes it's appropriate to allow our middle schoolers to learn from the natural consequences of their actions. For example, if Asanti's mother, Adanna, resisted asking her daughter whether she'd put her homework in her bag, Asanti would go to school without the homework. The result—either a reprimand from the teacher or a lower grade would be uncomfortable, and she'd likely learn from the natural consequences to take more care the next time. Sometimes, of course, natural consequences won't work. Hearken back to both Jordan and Kevin from Chapter 2, for whom the natural consequences weren't enough to break their cycles of disorganization. However, trying natural consequences can be an important first step, especially because they're such powerful teachers. Many parents are wary about allowing their children to experience the natural consequences of their actions—worrying that their child will "fail." And of course, we don't want that to happen.

But we're not talking about drowning here, and it's OK to let them sink a few times. Going to school without her homework once, or even twice, is unlikely to cause Asanti to flunk a class. As parents, though, we find it easy to project the worst-case scenario onto our children. We love them so much, and that love is often accompanied by fear that they won't reach their potential. So, the one time they neglect to turn in a piece of homework, we translate that to flunking out of school. The one time they lose their coat, we think it means they'll "never" be responsible.

The Natural Consequences Technique: It's OK to let your child sink sometimes.

The mistakes that our preteens make are an inevitable and integral part of the learning process. In *The Blessing of a Skinned Knee: Using Jewish Teachings to Raise Self-Reliant Children,* Wendy Mogel observes that parents behave as if we're cruise directors on a ship and our job is to make sure our children grow up with as few bumps as possible. She goes on to say that this is the worst possible mistake we can make. She asserts, "Our job is to raise our children to leave us. The children's job is to find their own path in life. If they stay carefully protected in the nest of the family, children will become weak and fearful or feel too comfortable to want to leave."

THE SANDWICH TECHNIQUE

Whenever possible, then, it's best to allow our preteen to experience the natural consequences of his or her choices. There are, of course, exceptions: when the consequences may be dangerous, or unhealthy, as in the case of Nick's not brushing his teeth, or when the natural consequences don't have an effect, as in the cases of Jordan and Kevin, then we as parents have a duty to step in.

How we do this involves first setting ourselves up for success. We've already seen that virtually the last thing to which middle schoolers will respond positively is the direct approach. In order to have them "hear" the importance of teeth brushing, we must present the problem to our children in a positive way. Mary Pipher, in her book *The Shelter of Each Other: Rebuilding Our Families,* recommends the "Sandwich Technique."

The "sandwich technique" is a communication skill that allows us to frame our values, concerns, even criticisms, in a way that our preteen can hear them without feeling defensive. The first step (the "bread" on the bottom of the sandwich) lies in formulating a positive statement to our child. For example, Samantha might say the following to Nick: "You know, Nick, I really appreciate how independent you're becoming. You've started taking a lot of responsibility in a number of areas."

The Sandwich Technique:
The first piece of bread is a positive, honest statement.

This first statement needn't be long, but it must be honest. Preteens have finely tuned radar for dishonesty or manipulation. If our middle schooler believes we're saying something only in order to manipulate him into behaving in a certain way, he will tune us out. If Samantha feels that she can't, in all honesty, say that Nick is becoming independent in other areas, she should formulate her first statement differently—perhaps by saying: "I know how much you hate my nagging, Nick, and I'm really trying to cut down. You're a trustworthy kid, and it's just going to take me a while to catch up to the 'new' and more grown-up Nick."

Some parents are surprised to discover that learning to formulate positive, honest statements can take practice. The good news is twofold, though: first, our children give us plenty of opportunities for practice; and second, much of their behavior is repetitive.

Script Yourself

Repetitive behavior gives us an advantage in that we can "script" ourselves in advance. Scripting involves being a "proactive" rather than a "reactive" parent. The difference between the two is that reactive parents wait for an issue to come up and then try to handle it on the spot. Proactive parents, on the other hand, think ahead and plan carefully so that their interventions and communications with their children are effective.

In Samantha and Nick's case, then, Samantha knows that the teeth-brushing problem is likely to occur every morning. This gives her the opportunity to create and memorize a script, based on the sandwich technique, and to sit down with Nick in the afternoon or evening to talk to him, when feelings are less likely to be running high.

The Script Technique:
Be proactive and use a "script" to get your point across.

"I Statements"

The next part of the script is the "meat" of the sandwich. Here is where we can express our concerns to our middle schooler. In the "meat" of the sandwich, it's important for us to take ownership of our concerns by using what's called an "I statement." These "I statements" reflect personal responsibility rather than pointing the finger of blame. They contrast sharply with "You statements," which will make the preteen *feel* defensive and angry.

Here are examples of both:

"I statement"	"You statement"
"I feel a little concerned about teeth brushing."	"You don't seem to be brushing your teeth in the morning."
"I'm confused about whether your homework is getting turned in on time."	"You aren't taking responsibility for your homework."
"I feel bewildered about what you just said."	"You're lying to me."

As you can see, "I statements" start with the word *I,* and "You statements" start with the word *you.* However, don't make the mistake of believing that just beginning a statement with the word *I* automatically makes it an "I statement." For example, "I think you're lying about brushing your teeth in the morning" is a "You statement" disguised as an "I statement." What differentiates the true "I statement" from the disguised "I statement" is that true "I statements" don't point the finger of blame; they take responsibility for our feelings about a situation. Thus, "I statements" must include a feeling word as well as beginning with a self-reference.

The Sandwich Technique:
The meat of the sandwich is "I statements."

FEELING WORDS

We create powerful "I statements" when we use the wealth of feeling words available to us, rather than sticking to what I call "umbrella feelings," the five or six common feeling words with which we are the most comfortable and that we use the most often. While you may have your own umbrella "set," here are the ones most people use: angry, sad, scared, overwhelmed, frustrated, upset, and happy.

The problem with using only umbrella feelings is that our children can become desensitized to them. After numerous "I statements" in which a parent says, "I feel upset that . . . the preteen is bound to think (or say), "Well, you're *always* upset, so what does it matter?"

It's far more effective to branch out, to use all of the various words that are available to us. Here is a list of possibilities:

Pleasant feelings		Unpleasant feelings	
calm	caring	bored	cautious
cheered	comfortable	cheated	concerned
confident	content	confused	cranky
creative	daring	defeated	defiant
delighted	eager	disappointed	discouraged
elated	encouraged	domineering	down
energetic	enthusiastic	embarrassed	envious
excited	fascinated	foolish	frustrated
free	full	guilty	hateful
glad	great	hesitant	hopeless
gutsy	happy	hurt	impatient
helpful	high	irritated	jealous
hopeful	humble	let-down	lonely
important	inspired	miserable	nervous
joyful	lovely	overwhelmed	overworked
loving	overjoyed	pained	possessive
peaceful	Peppy	pressured	provoked
playful	pleased	pushed	rejected
proud	refreshed	remorseful	resentful
relieved	satisfied	shy	skeptical
secure	snappy	stupid	suspicious
sophisticated	successful	threatened	tired
surprised	sympathetic	trapped	uncomfortable
tender	tranquil	uneasy	unhappy
understood	warm	unloved	unsure
wonderful	zany	weary	worried

Here are a few possibilities for Samantha's "I statement" to Nick:

> "One area that I feel concerned about is teeth brushing."
> "I'm unsure about whether you're brushing your teeth every morning.
>
> "I'm a little worried that you might be skipping your teeth brushing in the morning and developing cavities."

Avoid Using the Word But

As we cover the first piece of "bread" with the "meat of the sandwich," it's important that we not connect the two with the word *but*.

Connecting "bread" to "meat" the right way

"You know, Nick, I really appreciate how independent you're becoming. I'm a little worried that you might be skipping your teeth brushing in the morning and developing cavities."

Connecting "bread" to "meat" the wrong way

"You know, Nick, I really appreciate how independent you're becoming, but I'm a little worried that you might be skipping your teeth brushing in the morning and developing cavities."

The word *but* negates everything that comes before it. Thus, the child would hear the concern or criticism, but not the positive statement about his independence. This would put him on the defensive and be less effective.

PUTTING IT ALL TOGETHER

Once we formulate our "I statement," it's time to put the second piece of bread on the "sandwich." As with the first piece of bread, the second should be a positive statement, preferably one that projects trust about how things will go in the future.

The Sandwich Technique:
The second piece of bread is a positive statement
or statement of trust.

Samantha might say: "I'm sure we can work out a way that I can support your independence around this issue and stop nagging. What do you think?"

Notice how Samantha finishes with a question. This helps engage the preteen in the communication process and makes it more likely for him to take ownership of a solution, should one be reached. However, the question is not absolutely necessary to the "sandwich." Samantha could just as easily say, "I trust that you'll be self-reliant in this area, since you're already accepting responsibility in so many other ways."

EXHIBITING TRUST

Trust is a crucial part of the relationship between parent and middle schooler. If we act as though our preteen isn't trustworthy, then there's no reason for him to act responsibly. His thought will be, "Well, Mom/Dad doesn't trust me anyway, so why should I make an effort to be trusted?"

Exhibiting trust is often a matter of perspective. It's somewhat like seeing a glass as half full instead of half empty. When we're in doubt about whether our preteen is fulfilling a responsibility, or when she is "doing it right" at least some of the time, we want to use the skill of exhibiting trust to communicate our positive expectations.

Exhibiting Trust:
Calling the glass half full instead of half empty.

This brings us back to Adanna's question about Asanti, who asks to be trusted but then breaks trust by not doing what she says she has done. Adanna's first step with Asanti should be to use the sandwich technique. She might say:

[Bread] "Asanti, I really appreciate your growing desire for independence, and when I nag, it probably seems as if I don't trust you. Trust is important in our relationship, and I'm going to work on not nagging so I can show you how much I do trust you. [Meat] I can't help feeling a little concerned that your homework might not be getting into your schoolbag each morning, and that showing up without it will lead to lower grades than you deserve. [Bread] You're a good student, and I know that you'll take this responsibility seriously."

After Adanna has used the sandwich technique, she should quietly observe to see how Asanti is doing. At this point, it's critical that Adanna *stop nagging*. She needs to give Asanti a chance to either sink or prove herself. Any breach in exhibiting trust will serve as proof to Asanti that Adanna didn't really mean what she said and that she doesn't really trust her after all.

If Asanti does indeed "sink" once or twice, if she comes home bemoaning the teacher's "unfairness" in giving her a lower grade because she turned in a piece of homework after its deadline, it's imperative that Adanna refrain from saying, "I told you so." "I told you so" ruins natural consequences.

Instead of saying, "I told you so," Asanti could use "exhibiting trust": "How disappointing for you. I'm so sorry it worked out that way. You're a good student, though, Asanti, and I know that you'll figure out a way to get the grade you think you deserve."

"I told you so" ruins natural consequences. Use the "exhibiting trust" technique instead.

THE TRUST CONTRACT

What if after Asanti has sunk once or twice, however, it becomes apparent to Adanna that her daughter is beginning to drown? Then it's time to set up a "trust contract." With middle schoolers, it is essential to initially give trust freely, but once trust is broken, it then must be earned back.

Our children desperately want us to trust them. Loss of our trust represents a powerful consequence for inappropriate behavior. This is true, however, only if they've experienced the benefits of our trust in the past, which is why it's so important that, we give them our trust freely to begin with. If and only if they breach that trust should they then have to prove that they're trustworthy.

The first step in setting up a "trust contract" is to think through the following questions:

- **How much time is needed for our middle schooler to earn back our trust?**
- **What action can we take to ensure that trust isn't being broken?**

The amount of time required for a middle schooler to earn back trust, as well as what action we take, will often depend on the severity of the infraction. For example, one mother's son stole some items from cars in a parking lot. This is a serious infraction. She set up a period of two months for him to earn her trust back. Having a specific time line such as this is important. If the probationary period is ambiguous, the middle schooler will feel defeated, as if he's climbing a mountain with no end. If he feels defeated and becomes discouraged, he will likely give up and revert back to untrustworthy actions.

Set a reasonable time frame. Create a logical way for your preteen to earn back your trust.

The action that we decide on should be logically related to however the child has broken trust. As for the mother whose son vandalized cars, she curtailed his independence by walking him to and from school every day and accompanying him on any extracurricular activities that he had planned. Her rationale for this was that he hadn't behaved responsibly when she allowed him freedom and independence, so the result was that his freedom and independence would be decreased until she felt he was trustworthy once more. By creating this kind of logical relationship, we help our middle schoolers learn to evaluate the consequences and modify their behavior accordingly. For this mother and son, there were also times when the child's activities conflicted with her plans. Rather than follow him around like a puppy dog and inconvenience herself, she made him cancel his activities.

If Samantha needs to set up a trust contract for Nick's not brushing his teeth, any of the following actions would be logical:

- **Check his toothbrush every morning to see if it's wet.**
- **Check his teeth every morning to make sure they look clean.**
- **Schedule a dental appointment at the end of the week to have the dentist determine whether proper hygiene is being maintained.**

If Adanna needs to set up a trust contract for Asanti's not putting her homework in her bag, she might decide to use one of the following logically related actions:

- **Check Asanti's bag each morning to make sure the homework is there.**
- **Ask Asanti's teacher to send her an e-mail every day to report about whether the homework is present.**
- **Supervise every evening so that she sees Asanti putting the homework in her bag.**

Clearly, the issues that Samantha and Adanna are having with their middle schoolers are not anywhere near as serious as breaking into cars and stealing. Therefore, each might set up a period of one week or less for her preteen to earn back trust.

PRESENTING THE TRUST CONTRACT

Equally important to the content of the contract is the method of presentation. Trust contracts are not meant to punish or control our children, but rather to engage our children in a relationship with us so that we can support them in growing up. Trust should always be viewed and communicated as a valued commodity in the household. The more responsible you are, the more trust you engender.

When we present the trust contract to our children, it's important to come from a relationship perspective. This means utilizing some of the techniques you've learned thus far: "I statements," "sandwiching," and "scripting."

For example, Adanna might script herself during the day and approach Asanti on the weekend:

> ["I statement"] "Asanti, I feel extremely concerned about the fact that I've trusted you to put your homework in your bag and you've now forgotten three times. [Bread of sandwich] I believe that this is something you can remember to do without my nagging. [Meat of sandwich] I'm going to ask you to earn my trust back in this regard, [Bread of sandwich] which I'm sure that you can do, because you're a trustworthy kid. [Length of time] For the next three days, [Action] I'm going to check your bag every morning to make sure your work is there. [Garnish!] At the end of that time, I know you'll prove to me that you're trustworthy, and my trust in you will be restored. At that point I'll stop checking.

Sometimes parents worry that using the script technique makes them sound phony. This is understandable. Remember that as a parent of a preteen, you're essentially learning a new language to deal with the "foreigner" in your house. If you were learning Russian, Chinese, or any other language that's new to you, you would sound stilted and insecure at first. You would need to practice the phrases you were learning over and over again to "get it right" and make it sound smooth and natural. It would take time for you to become fluent. The same is true of your communication techniques with your middle schooler.

Remember that learning a new "language" takes time. It may sound "phony" to you at first.

If you're worried that your child will think you're odd for speaking in this new way, there's no problem with presenting it to him by saying something like, "I'm learning a new way to speak to you respectfully that will honor your growing independence. It's new to me, though, and it might sound funny for a while. I hope you'll be patient as I learn."

Wrapping It Up by "Acknowledging Effort"

Finally, it's important to acknowledge when our children are making progress. This act of "acknowledging effort" should be performed both during and at the end of the trust contract.

Use "acknowledging effort" throughout your parenting to encourage your preteen's step-by-step progress.

Thus, Samantha and Adanna should make sure to acknowledge progress during the length of time that the contract is in place. Samantha might say, "You're doing a great job restoring my trust. Only two more days to go."

When trust is restored in full, this should be acknowledged as well: "I knew you could do it. You've regained my full trust. Great work."

HOW'D THEY DO?

Let's hear how the parents and preteens in this chapter finally worked things out.

SAMANTHA AND NICK

Samantha approached Nick without feeling the need to script herself. She chose to time her intervention when Nick's basketball team had just won an important game and Nick was feeling especially proud of his contribution.

She used the sandwich technique and said, "You know, this is just one more example of how competent you're becoming, Nick. You must feel so proud of yourself, just as I feel proud of you too. And I know this seems completely out of the blue, but I've noticed that I've been nagging you about certain things, and I realize that I just don't need to do that so much anymore. It'll take me a while to get used to it, but I'm going to make a start and stop nagging you about brushing your teeth in the mornings. I know that you don't need me to do that and that you'll be as competent in that as you are in so many other ways."

Nick looked surprised and said, "Well, thanks, Mom."

Samantha spent the next week observing, and she reported that while Nick didn't brush his teeth every morning, he managed five out of seven days, which was much better than before. She then used "acknowledging effort" by saying, "I have to tell you I noticed that you remembered to brush your teeth without my nagging this week."

While it may have been tempting for Samantha to mention that Nick missed two days, she resisted being a perfectionist and was satisfied with the fact that Nick had made progress. Sure enough, her trust that the progress would continue paid off, and in the second week and beyond, Nick became entirely responsible and brushed his teeth every morning.

ADANNA AND ASANTI

Adanna had a tougher time with Asanti. Because Asanti's general nature is more defiant than Nick's, Adanna felt she needed to "cut to the chase" and begin with a trust contract. She spent several days working out a script that felt comfortable and decided that when she sat down with Asanti, she would have some "cues" written down to help her remember how she wanted to phrase the contract.

She said, "Asanti, I realize that you're getting older and that I may still be treating you like a much younger child. I don't want to do that anymore, and my guess is that you don't want me to do that either."

Asanti nodded but looked suspicious as her mother continued.

"I know I've been nagging you about putting your homework in your bag every night. I'd like to trust that you can do that yourself. What I want to do is set up a sort-of 'trust contract' with you . . ."

Asanti broke in: "You *don't* trust me. I've been trying to tell you that. You *never* believe *anything* I say I'm going to do."

Adanna took a deep breath and, utilizing the "listening with heart" skill from Chapter 1, said, "Tell me what you mean."

Asanti's eyes narrowed and her tone became sarcastic. "Tell me what you mean," she said, her voice mimicking her mother. "I'll *tell* you what I mean. I *tell* you over and over again that I'm going to put my homework in my bag. And then you ask me *again*. And I tell you I'm not done, but do you hear that? NO0000. You're always so focused on making sure everything is under control that you *never* hear a word I say and you *never* trust me."

It would have been easy for Adanna to take Asanti's "bait"—the sarcastic tone she used when she mimicked her mother's words. To Adanna's credit, however, she didn't bite; instead, she continued to "listen with heart." She'd already discovered that "hugging a porcupine" isn't easy but that sometimes it's the best way to achieve our goals.

Hugging a porcupine isn't easy.

Avoid "rising to the bait."

"Wow, Asanti," Adanna said with concern, "I guess I didn't realize that I was being so controlling. I'd like to stop doing that."

"Yeah?" Asanti sneered. "How?"

"Well, I'm not exactly sure, because I've never done this before. What about if we make a deal? I'll promise that I won't ask you for an entire week about your homework, and we'll see how it goes, and you'll promise to 'meet' with me at the end of the week to give me feedback from your perspective."

"What happens if I say no?" Asanti asked.

"Well, nothing. I guess we just go back to the old way of doing things, with me nagging and both of us being unhappy."

Asanti thought for a moment and then said grudgingly, "Well, OK, I'll try it. But if you nag me, then I'm not meeting."

"That sounds fair," Adanna replied.

Notice that while the process was interrupted because of Asanti's defiance and anger, Adanna still got her "trust contract" communicated, albeit in a slightly different form from the one she originally intended. In addition, she didn't allow herself to be distracted from her goal by Asanti's challenging attitude, which was probably deliberate on Asanti's part. No doubt Asanti hoped that by distracting or angering her mother, she could avoid having the conversation altogether.

At the end of the week, Asanti had managed to get her homework in her bag twice but suffered "natural consequences" at school on two of the other mornings. Because Adanna kept her end of the trust bargain and didn't say anything, Asanti felt free to express her disappointment about her consequences when they met at the end of the week.

"I can't believe that I forgot to put my homework in my bag. The teacher lowered my grade *and* gave me extra work to do to make up for it. I guess I did better when you nagged me."

Adanna refused to buy into Asanti's negative attitude. Instead, she replied by "acknowledging effort": "No, you did remember some of the time. I'm sorry that you have extra work to do, but I'm sure it won't happen again. I know that you can do it."

"Thanks, Mom," Asanti replied. "I hope so."

By not allowing Asanti to slip into a negative state of mind ("I did better when you nagged me"), Adanna was able to break out of the nagging cycle of distrust in which they'd been engaged. The following week, she again kept her mouth shut, and Asanti remembered her homework every day.

THE BOY WHO BROKE INTO CARS

Believe it or not, there was no fight about earning back parental trust in this case. Mom presented the trust contract matter-of-factly and unemotionally, and her son allowed her to accompany him to school and to his extracurricular activities for the two-month period. At the end of that time, Mom communicated that trust had been restored. Four years have now passed, and the boy has not done anything like that again. In fact, he is a responsible teen who works as a camp counselor with younger children each summer and is a trusted and valued member of the camp community.

Family meetings can be a great way to build trust and communication as our kids grow more independent. And if they are handled carefully and consistently as **JULIE ROSS** show us in this piece, they can become cornerstones in an otherwise chaotic family life. And at The Parents Union we agree with Julie's assertion that in order to be truly effective parents, "we must have a larger sense of purpose for everything we do." As she says, "It's not enough to simply address concerns as they come up. We must also take the "long view" of parenting."

Taking the long view, building trust and establishing consistent family meetings can really transform what some call the urgency of the immediate and help us move from being re-active parents to pro-active ones.

—Marc Sachnoff, Chief Parent, The Parents Union

WHAT ARE FAMILY MEETINGS?

F amily meetings are a practical tool for encouraging family cohesion during middle school and beyond. Basically, they comprise a short amount of distraction-free time that you set aside weekly to be together as a family. They give you the opportunity to discuss values and other relevant issues, to make decisions, to problem solve, and to reinforce a sense of "family community" in an emotion-neutral zone.

WHY BOTHER?

Initially, you might wonder what could possibly be gained from scheduling one more task into your already busy life! After all, you might think, you can make decisions and problem solve on an ad hoc basis. And clearly, you role-model values to your family daily.

Why, then, should you set aside twenty to forty-five minutes of your valuable time weekly to do what you're essentially already doing?

I believe that to be truly effective parents, we must have a larger sense of purpose for everything we do. It's not enough to simply address concerns as they come up. We must also take the "long view" of parenting that we talked about in Chapter 1: asking ourselves not only, "Is what I'm doing 'working'?" (in other words, "Am I getting by?") but also, "What am I teaching to and providing for my child: am I meeting my child's needs?"

Family meetings teach our children to communicate, brainstorm, and problem solve in a group setting. In addition, they provide our children with the opportunity to contribute to something that's bigger and more important than they are. In turn, this helps them achieve a universal need of all human beings: to belong.

When our children feel as though they're making a meaningful contribution to the family "community," and when they know that the family is a place where they will *always* fit in and belong, it reduces the risk that they will reject family in favor of peer group as they grow.

> All human beings need to feel that we belong and are making a meaningful contribution to something that's bigger and more important than we are.

MAKING IT WORK

There are several guidelines that I recommend you follow to help ensure that your family meetings run smoothly. The first is to hold your family meetings on the same day and at the same time each week. This consistency is indispensable in a busy household. Without it, it's all too easy to allow something else to take priority and let family meetings go by the wayside.

Next, you need to create an agenda and post it in a convenient place where family members can write down topics they'd like to discuss or problems they'd like to brainstorm about at the next meeting. This shows your middle schooler that you're taking the idea of her contribution seriously and helps her feel integral to the family.

It's also essential to have a format for your meetings. A format keeps the goings-on orderly so that chaos doesn't ensue, with family members talking over one another so as to have their opinions heard. While any format that you might choose would probably be just fine as long as it's consistent, many families have experienced success using the following breakdown:

- **Compliment one another. (Compliments set the tone for the meetings.)**
- **Review anything that didn't get resolved at the last meeting. Talk about new issues or decisions that need to be addressed as a family.**
- **Hand out allowances.**
- **Close the meeting with something fun—a game, a hug, ice cream . . . it can be different every time.**

Use the skills of "tell me more," "listening with heart" and "cooperative communication" throughout your meetings. Remember that family meetings are supposed to help your children feel a sense of belonging. If the sessions are used for criticism and condemnation of behaviors, you won't accomplish this purpose.

THE FAMILY MEETING IN ACTION

When Jeanne complains again about having such an early bedtime, Ruth "listens with heart" and says: "You know, I have an idea. I don't want to just arbitrarily say no to you about this, because I recognize that it's important to you. Why don't we sit down with Dad and Aaron later, and we can all discuss it?"

Later, Ruth; her husband, Dave; Jeanne; and Jeanne's nine-year-old brother, Aaron, sit down for their first family meeting.

"OK, gang," Ruth announces, "I think it's best if we have a format for our meetings so that everyone who wants to say something gets a turn. Let's start by complimenting one another. Then, if anyone has anything he or she would like to bring up, we can talk about it.

Also, I thought it would be good to give you guys your allowances during family meeting each week; that way, we won't forget to do it! What do you think?"

Aaron punches the air and exclaims, "All right, allowance!" Jeanne sits slumped in her chair, one elbow on the table and her head in her hand. "Fine," she mutters, rolling her eyes.

Ruth wisely chooses to ignore Jeanne's body language and moves on. "OK, well, I'd like to compliment you, Dave, on finishing your big project at work." She turns to Aaron: "Aaron, I want to compliment you on working so hard on your science fair project, and Jeanne, I want to compliment you on being at this meeting even though I know you have your doubts about it." Jeanne looks uncomfortable but doesn't say anything. "Now, who'd like to go next?"

Each family member should take a turn complimenting every other family member. Starting with compliments may initially feel forced and stilted, but you'll discover that it soon becomes more natural and is often the part of the meeting to which everyone looks forward the most.

"Now," Ruth says, "does anyone have anything you'd like to talk about on the agenda today?"

"Mom," Jeanne says impatiently, "give me a break! You said we were going to have a discussion so we could talk about my bedtime, and now it's all formal and stuff. Can't we just go already?"

"I know, Jeanne," Ruth acknowledges, "and we can talk about

bedtime first if you want. But I would like for us to make these discussions a habit, and I want everyone to feel included. Now, why don't you go first?"

"Mom, you *know* what I want. Come *on!*"

Jeanne's impatience is normal. Until your middle schooler realizes that these meetings can be beneficial to her, she may resist them. Be patient and persevere.

"OK, Jeanne, I know you want a later bedtime . . . "

"I want a later bedtime too!" Aaron shouts.

"Shut up," Jeanne says, glaring at him. "This isn't about you; it's about me."

"MOOOOmmmmm!" Aaron protests.

Ruth holds up her hands. "Ground rule number one: everyone gets a chance to talk and make requests, but not all at once. If you're worried you'll forget what you want to say, write it down, but if you interrupt, your turn will be taken away. First we're going to focus on Jeanne."

"Ha!" Jeanne shouts, making a face at her brother. "OK, I don't want to go to bed so early. All my friends have a later bedtime, and you treat me like a baby."

Jeanne's father decides to use the skill of "tell me more." He asks her, "So, what time do your friends go to bed?"

Seeing a potential ally, Jeanne turns to him and replies, "Daddy, they go to bed when they want, like really late. Like 11:00. And you guys make me go to bed at 9:00, and it's just not fair."

Dave prods, "So, I'm curious as to what they're doing with that extra time?"

"Well, homework and stuff."

"So, they're using the extra time to do homework, and . . . ?" "Well, I dunno, probably IMing or relaxing, or reading or something."

> Don't rush the discussion. Slowing down
> will achieve more.

"What do you think you would use the extra time for?"

"I dunno. I just feel like you're treating me like a baby."

As Dave pursues a course of getting Jeanne to tell him more, Ruth is listening with heart and interjects: "So, it sounds as if you feel out of sync with your friends, as if maybe they're being treated as more grown up than you are."

"That's right, Mom, and I'm old enough too."

"Well," Dave says, "I think we can believe you're old enough to have a later bedtime. We realize that you're growing up, Jeanne. And as you continue to get older, we'll probably have to re-discuss the rules that we've set for you, so we appreciate your willingness to talk about this with us."

Ruth then engages the quality of reciprocity—acknowledging both Jeanne's need as well as Dave's and her need:

Speaking for them both, Ruth says: "We hear that you feel the need for a later bedtime. What we need is to know that you are getting enough sleep to be able to function well at school." She continues by engaging the quality of collaboration and using the skill of "cooperative communication": "What do you think we can do so that you get what you need and so that we feel reassured that you're getting enough sleep?"

Cooperative Communication:
> Respect and acknowledge feelings.
> Brainstorm solutions.
> Create a plan that meets everyone's needs.

The discussion continues, with the end result being that they will move Jeanne's bedtime incrementally and assess weekly whether her schoolwork is suffering.

The first week, they move her bedtime from 9:00 to 9:30. At the next family meeting, they agree that a 9:30 bedtime went well and they will move the bedtime again—this time to 10:00. Again, at the end of the week, it's determined that Jeanne is handling the later time well and they will try 10:30. At the following meeting, though, it's clear that 10:30 has not worked so well. Even Jeanne agrees that she feels tired in the mornings after having gone to bed so late. As a family, they decide to push Jeanne's bedtime back to 10:00 for the time being, with the provision that the discussion can be reopened at a later date by either Jeanne or her parents if things aren't going well.

Ruth and Dave do an impressive job here, allowing Jeanne to experience the natural consequences of a later bedtime and come to the decision that no matter what time her friends are going to bed, the appropriate time for her as an individual is 10:00 P.M.

Natural consequences can work in your favor.

For Jeanne, the positive outcome of getting a later bedtime reinforced the notion that family meetings weren't such a bad idea. Getting her allowance on a regular basis didn't hurt either!

Can Family Meetings Fail?

My favorite story about the challenges that can arise with family meetings was told to me by the father of three boys. They had initiated family meetings several months before, and both parents thought the meetings were going well. One day, however, only the youngest boy showed up at the appointed time. Five minutes passed; then ten. Dad began to feel annoyed. "Boys!" he shouted. "You're holding up the meeting! What's going on up there?"

"We're coming!" There was a rustling noise. Something fell, hitting the floor with a thunk. Then, silence. Another five minutes passed. Just as Dad was about to lose his cool, both boys appeared at the top of the staircase. Marching slowly down the stairs and then around the living room, each boy carried an elaborately let-tered sign: "On Strike with Family Meetings!"

Family meetings rarely "fail," but sometimes they need to be adjusted so that everyone sees the benefit. If your child "goes on strike," reexamine the four qualities necessary in a relationship approach: respect, support, reciprocity, and collaboration. Put yourself in your child's shoes: If you were the child at the meeting, would you look forward to coming? Would you feel respected and supported? Would it feel as though there was a spirit of collaboration at the meeting? Would you feel listened to? Or would you worry that it was just a session in which your parents could complain about the things you were doing wrong?

The most significant outcome of any family meeting is that each child feels "heard" and respected. Even when you make a decision that your middle schooler doesn't like or agree with, if she feels that family meetings are a forum in which you "listen with heart" and she can raise issues without being criticized, she will continue to attend and be less likely to rebel.

To this end, it's best to use the first few family meetings specifically as a forum for your middle schooler and other children to voice their issues or requests. When possible, say yes or maybe to what they want, in order to reinforce the benefit of the meetings. If you must say no to a request, remember that it will elicit less rebellion if it's conditional or temporary—for example: "I'm not comfortable with that right now, but we can rediscuss it in a few weeks," or "I'm not sure I can say yes to you just yet; I'll write it down, and we'll bring it up after your next birthday." Even having to postpone a decision for a year feels less restrictive to a middle schooler than an outright "No, never!"

Finally, no one should be forced to attend family meetings. If your middle schooler chooses not to attend, have the meeting anyway—unless, of course, you're a single parent of one child. If that's the case, simply emphasize that no meeting means no allowance, since that's the time when it's handed out. Even for noncompliant middle schoolers, once they realize that nonattendance means no allowance, they'll choose to come. And once they've started to attend, they'll eventually discover that having a say in family decisions is better than having decisions made without their input.

5

WHAT YOU NEED TO KNOW ABOUT THE TYPES OF SCHOOLS

We are indebted to **DR. BRYAN AND EMILY HASSEL** for generously making available sections of their excellent book, the *Picky Parent Guide: Choose Your Child's School with Confidence.* In this piece you'll find information about the different types of schools, how to determine if a school is a good fit for your child based on what they call the four "Fit Factors" and a simple checklist to help you pull it all together so you can make the best decision for each of your kids while taking into account your family's needs.

—Marc Sachnoff, Chief Parent, The Parents Union

GET SMART ABOUT SCHOOL TYPES

(The following excerpts are from *Picky Parent Guide: Choose You Child's School with Confidence,* p. 7)

Many parents make broad, sweeping assumptions about whether one *type* of school will offer better quality for their children. In fact, when parental education and income are factored out, research has not consistently shown that any one type of school educates children better than other types. (You might also be interested in school designs, such as Montessori, Core Knowledge and the like.) Still, it's good to know about the different types of school that may be in your community:

> *District public schools* typically are funded mainly through a combination of local, state and federal funding, "owned" by the public, and controlled by the local board of education.

Magnet schools are also public schools, but typically have a special curriculum or teaching method. They draw from a cross-section of a city or town rather than specific neighborhoods.

Special programs within schools. More and more schools run special programs for a subset of students, such as foreign language and International Baccalaureate programs.

Charter schools are also public and in most states are funded with a combination of local, state and federal money, but they are "owned" and controlled by independent groups of citizens. They can lose their public funding if they do not meet performance goals.

Private independent schools are funded mainly through a combination of tuition and fees charged to parents and fundraising campaigns, owned by nonprofit organizations (although not always), and controlled by boards of alumni, parents, staff and interested citizens.

Private religious schools typically are funded through a combination of tuition and fees, fundraising campaigns and money from a larger religious body. They are owned by nonprofit entities and controlled by boards mostly made up of people whose religious affiliations match the schools.

Home schooling means teaching your child at home, either alone or in conjunction with other home-schooling parents. You own, you control, and—in most areas—you pay for materials and equipment.

(from *Picky Parent Guide: Choose You Child's School with Confidence*, p. 7)

FOCUS ON THE FOUR FIT FACTORS

Great Fit Triangle

Matching Child and Family Needs with
School Offerings

Child Needs

What: Basic Learning Capability • other capabilities • interests

How: Learning styles • motivation • physical, mental health • behavioral challenges • disabilities and disorders • self-understanding

Social Issues: Friends at school

Practical Matters: Essential activities

School Offerings

What: Mission • education goals • curriculum content • extracurriculars

How: Teaching methods • classroom discipline • communications with parents • mental and physical health care resources • offerings for students with disorders and disabilities • culture of school

Social Issues: Parent community • parent involvement • student community

Practical Matters: Activities accommodated • schedule • child care • transportation • location • multiple children's needs met • cost

Family Needs

What: Values about content • goals for child

How: Values about student conduct rules • teaching method • classroom discipline • your role as advocate for child

Social Issues: Parent community • parent involvement • student community • preference for school, type or design

Practical Matters: Child care needs • schedule • transportation • location • your other children • money available for schooll

Some school differences affect school quality, some affect fit with child and family needs, and some affect both. Here, we are focusing on school differences that affect fit.

So how can you, the parent, make sense of the jumble of characteristics you see when you begin to investigate schools? As with your child and family *needs*, you can use our four Fit Factors to understand how one school's *offerings* differ from another's:

What Your Child Learns: Schools differ greatly in their overall educational "mission," which is a statement of what a school aims to accomplish and why. Schools also vary in the range of subjects taught, how challenging the educational goals are for each child, and extracurricular offerings.

How Your Child Learns: Schools differ in how teachers instruct students, both in their main approaches used for all students and alternative approaches used for students with particular needs and challenges. Schools vary in their disciplinary policies and practices (in and out of the classroom) and the overall culture of interaction between the school, students, and parents.

Social Issues: When you choose a school, you're choosing a unique group of kids and adults with whom you and your child will spend time. Social Issues include the school's social norms and values as well as the characteristics of its students and parents. The types and levels of parent participation in the school community are part of this Factor, too.

Practical Matters: Each school has its own daily and annual schedule, transportation system, and location. Some offer before and after school care, some don't. Some are free of charge, others charge anywhere from a lot to a little in tuition.

(from *Picky Parent Guide: Choose You Child's School with Confidence*, p. 163)

WHERE DO I LOOK FOR INFORMATION ABOUT SCHOOLS?

You can get additional information about your Target Schools from a variety of sources, including those listed below.

Your state department of education. All states issue "report cards" on public schools or at least have lists and contact information available. To date, much of this information has gone unused by most parents. But it can be a good way to compare past performance in the basic subjects. You can compare individual schools, as well as towns and cities if you are considering a move. Try your state's website first to get information quickly.

Your local public school district's central office (look in the phone book). Your district should have information about school assignments, magnet schools, choices available among other public schools and the educational approach taken by various schools from which you may choose. Look for a website, which may have useful school performance numbers. Charter schools may not be included in information you get from your school district.

Individual schools

Staff: The principal, teachers and other staff should be available by appointment to help you. Receptionists may be able to answer practical questions about school hours, transportation, costs, child care, etc., but reserve questions about the classroom for other staff.

*Written materials:*Ask for anything that explains the school's mission, curriculum, teaching method, student population and other features of interest to you.

Tours and open houses: Use these as opportunities to find out all you can about the school. Ask questions. Make sure you ask about quality and fit Must Haves, so you can eliminate schools that are a clear "no." Write down what you hear and see. Many schools will throw heaps of irrelevant information your way, often highlighting offerings having little to do with quality and addressing fit only for a few. Warm cookies, flashy performances and scripted student recitations have wooed many a well-meaning parent to the wrong school. Filter out the flash, unless it truly addresses your child's or family's needs. Focus on *real* quality and your own child and family fit concerns. (But do enjoy the cookies.)

Observation: Reserve this for schools on your final list, as meaningful observations are time-consuming. Consider observing the grade your child would attend next year, as well as an older grade. Ideally, you would observe more than one teacher in each grade. When you observe, look for children who act like you expect yours would in the classroom. For example, if your child is very shy and quiet, observe whether teachers encourage the quiet ones to participate and give them time to respond. If your child will be the one with a hundred questions and comments, observe whether teachers act appreciative of enthusiastic children while also teaching them to focus their comments on main ideas.

Web site: search for a school's site on the internet or simply ask if the school has one. These often contain practical information as well as philosophy and educational approach. Pay attention to what they do not say, as well as what they do say.

Parents. One of your most valuable sources will be parents who have either child or family needs very similar to yours. In general, talking with parents of children *like yours* is as accurate a read on the experience your child would have as — and much more time efficient than — limited classroom observations.

As you talk with parents, make sure that you follow up with a quick question about their child and family needs. This will help you put their opinions into perspective. Asking parents of highly gifted children about their experience may not tell you whether a school would drive home the basics in reading, writing and math for your more typical child. Asking parents of a highly visual child who loves to sit, look and listen in her traditional school will not tell you how your bustling, kinesthetic child would fare. In short: understand the perspectives of your sources before taking opinion as fact.

A CONFIDENT CHOICE Tool

Personalized Great Fit Checklist

School Name: _____

➤ In the first blank column, list in pencil the precise names of your top child & family needs based on your *Child and Family Needs Summaries* (pages 38 and 110) and on your reading of Chapters 2–9 and related tables. For example, write: "Basic Learning Capability, Typical." See a complete example on page 176.

➤ ➤ Check whether each of your needs is a Must Have or Nice to Have.

➤ ➤ In next big column, make note of the characteristics a school must have to meet your need based on your reading of Chapter 10 and related tables.

➤ Include specific questions to ask school principal, teachers, parents, and others (or use our *Interview Forms* on page 273).

➤ ➤ Make an extra copy and fill in notes for each school you consider.

➤ ➤ After you gather the information you need, grade each school on how well it fits each Must Have and Nice to Have item:

A perfect fit   **C** halfway fit

B very good fit   **D** poor fit   **F** very poor or no fit

FIT FACTOR	CHILD & FAMILY NEEDS: Must Haves & top Nice to Haves	MUST HAVE	NICE TO HAVE	WHAT TO LOOK FOR *and* QUESTIONS TO ASK	NOTES ABOUT THIS SCHOOL	GRADE
What Your Child Learns						
How Your Child Learns						
Social Issues						
Practical Matters						

6

WHAT CHILDREN LEARN AND WHEN THEY LEARN IT

LEARNING GOALS

For Washington State

(from the Washington State Office of Superintendent
of Public Instruction)

Washington state established four learning goals, listed here, that apply to all grade levels and provide the foundation for the development of the Essential Academic Learning Requirements (EALRs), which help measure progress and accountability:

1. Read with comprehension, write with skill, and communicate effectively and responsibly in a variety of ways and settings.

2. Know and apply core concepts and principles of math, science, the arts, social studies, health and fitness.

3. Think analytically, logically and creatively, and integrate experience and knowledge to form reasoned judgments and solve problems.

4. Understand the importance of work and how performance, effort and decisions directly affect future career and educational opportunities.

Each grade has specific learning goals. Washington state has learning standards that define the knowledge and skills students should gain, starting with kindergarten. To learn more, go to www.k12.us/standards.

LEARNING GOALS BY GRADE LEVEL

Grade K

WRITING
- Knows that an audience exists outside of self and understands writing has different purposes
- Analyzes ideas, selects topics and adds details
- Knows and applies spelling, punctuation, capitalization, grammar and paragraphing appropriate to the grade level

READING
- Recognizes, understands and applies concepts of print and sounds
- Expands oral language skills and gains meaningful vocabulary for reading
- Demonstrates comprehension by responding in different ways when listening to or viewing text of all kinds
- Shows interest in a variety of books

MATH
- Begins to develop basic notions of numbers and uses numbers to think about objects and the world around them
- Learns what it means to add and subtract by joining and separating sets of objects
- Learns to describe attributes of geometric shapes, such as triangles, rectangles and circles

SCIENCE
- Learns that scientific investigations involve trying to answer questions by making observations or trying things out

- Learns to use simple tools (e.g., pencils, scissors) and materials (e.g., paper, tape, glue and cardboard) to solve problems in creative ways
- Learns about the properties of liquids and solids, objects seen in the sky and the needs of plants and animals

Grade 1

WRITING

- Knows that an audience exists outside of self and understands writing has different purposes
- Analyzes ideas, selects topics, adds details and elaborates
- Knows and applies spelling, punctuation, capitalization, grammar and paragraphing appropriate to the grade level

READING

- Applies concepts of print, sounds, oral language skills and phonics
- Continues to expand reading vocabulary and demonstrates comprehension by participating in a variety of responses to text
- Chooses and reads a variety of books for pleasure

MATH

- Develops understanding of addition and subtraction and strategies for adding and subtracting within 20
- Develops understanding of whole number relationships and place value
- Begins to understand what it means to measure something and develops measuring skills using everyday objects

SCIENCE

- Learns that scientific investigations involve trying to answer questions by making observations or trying things out
- Learns to use simple tools (e.g., pencils, scissors) and materials (e.g., paper, tape, glue and cardboard) to solve problems in creative ways
- Learns about the properties of liquids and solids, objects seen in the sky and the needs of plants and animals

Grade 2

WRITING

- Writes for a variety of audiences and purposes, including telling a story and explaining
- Analyzes ideas, selects topics, adds detail and elaborates
- Knows and applies spelling, punctuation, capitalization, grammar and paragraphing appropriate to the grade level

READING

- Becomes fluent as a reader, expands vocabulary, understands many different kinds of text and applies comprehension strategies
- Participates in discussions, writes responses and uses evidence from text to support thinking
- Continues making reading an enjoyable habit

MATH

- Refines understanding of the base ten number system and uses place value concepts of ones, tens and hundreds to understand number relationships
- Builds fluency with addition and subtraction
- Uses measurement tools to understand units of measure

SCIENCE

- Learns to think systematically about how the parts of objects, plants and animals are connected and work together
- Carries out investigations in collaboration with other students and support from the teacher
- Learns to identify different physical properties of materials, how water shapes landforms and the life cycles of plants and animals

Grade 3

WRITING

- Writes for a variety of audiences and purposes, including telling a story and explaining
- Analyzes ideas, selects topics, adds detail and elaborates
- Knows and applies spelling, punctuation, capitalization, grammar and paragraphing appropriate to the grade level

READING

- Reads fluently with meaning and purpose while expanding vocabulary
- Reads a wider variety of topics and genres
- Demonstrates comprehension of main ideas and details through discussion, writing and evidence from text to support thinking
- Reads for pleasure and chooses books based on personal preference, topic or author

MATH

- Develops understanding of multiplication and division and how they relate

- Develops understanding of fractions
- Develops understanding of area and its connection to multiplication by comparing them and representing them in different ways
- Uses pictures, symbols or math language to explain the reasoning behind their decisions and solutions

SCIENCE

- Learns to think systematically about how the parts of objects, plants and animals are connected and work together
- Carries out investigations in collaboration with other students and support from the teacher
- Learns to identify different physical properties of materials, how water shapes landforms, and the life cycles of plants and animals

Grade 4

WRITING

- Writes for a variety of audiences and purposes, including telling a story and explaining
- Analyzes ideas, selects a narrow topic and elaborates using specific details and/or examples
- Knows and applies spelling, punctuation, capitalization, grammar and paragraphing appropriate to the grade level

READING

- Reads skillfully with meaning and purpose, using appropriate comprehension and vocabulary strategies
- Reads, discusses, reflects and responds, using evidence from text, to a wide variety of literary genres and informational text

- Reads for pleasure and chooses books based on personal preference, topic or author

MATH
- Develops fluency with multiplication
- Uses multiplication to solve a variety of problems such as area and unit conversion
- Understands division and its relationship to multiplication
- Solidifies understanding of equal fractions and begins operations with fractions

SCIENCE
- Learns how to plan and choose an investigation based on the question they are trying to answer
- Uses an elementary technological design process to design simple solutions to problems
- Learns how energy is generated and can move from place to place, how fossils form and how ecosystems change

Grade 5

WRITING
- Writes for a variety of audiences and purposes, including persuading and explaining
- Analyzes ideas, selects a narrow topic and elaborates using specific details and/or examples
- Knows and applies spelling, punctuation, capitalization, grammar and paragraphing appropriate to the grade level

READING
- Reflects on skills and adjusts comprehension and vocabulary strategies to become better readers

- Reads, discusses, reflects and responds, using evidence from text to a wide variety of literary genres and informational text
- Reads for pleasure and chooses books based on personal preference, topic, genre, theme or author

MATH

- Develops fluency with division
- Develops understanding of decimal place value
- Develops understanding of the four operations on fractions and decimals
- Develops fluency with geometric concepts of area and perimeter

SCIENCE

- Learns how to plan and choose an investigation based on the question they are trying to answer
- Uses an elementary technological design process to design simple solutions to problems
- Learns how energy is generated and can move from place to place, how fossils form, and how ecosystems change

Grade 6

WRITING

- Writes for a variety of audiences and purposes, including persuading and explaining
- Analyzes ideas, selects a manageable topic and elaborates using specific, relevant details and/or examples
- Knows and applies spelling, punctuation, capitalization, grammar and paragraphing appropriate to the grade level

READING

- Adjusts reading purpose, pace and strategies according to difficulty and/or type of text
- Reads, discusses, reflects and responds with deeper analysis, using evidence from text to a wide variety of literary genres and informational text
- Reads for pleasure and chooses books based on personal preference, topic, genre, theme or author

MATH

- Extends division to fractions
- Extends understanding of numbers to negative numbers and the absolute value of a number
- Develops understanding of how letters (variables) are used to represent numbers in a variety of situations
- Use multiplication and division reasoning to solve real-world ratio and rate problems

SCIENCE

- Learns to think critically and logically to make connections between prior science knowledge and evidence produced from their investigations
- Learns to apply the full process of technological design, combined with relevant science concepts, to solve problems
- Learns how energy and matter interact, how the water cycle functions, and how inherited variations can become adaptations to a changing environment

Grade 7

WRITING
- Writes for a variety of audiences and purposes, including persuading and explaining
- Analyzes ideas, selects a manageable topic and elaborates using specific, relevant details and/or examples
- Knows and applies spelling, punctuation, capitalization, grammar and paragraphing appropriate to the grade level

READING
- Demonstrates responsibility as a reader, and continues to reflect on skills and adjust comprehension, analysis and vocabulary strategies
- Summarizes information from multiple sources to deepen understanding of the content in oral and written responses
- Reads for pleasure and chooses books based on personal preference, topic, genre, theme or author

MATH
- Adds, subtracts, multiplies and divides both positive and negative fractions, decimals and percents
- Solves real-world problems using simple expressions, equations and inequalities that include variables
- Extends work with ratios to solve problems involving proportional relationships and percents, like those found in similar figures, discounts and tips

SCIENCE
- Learns to think critically and logically to make connections between prior science knowledge and evidence produced from their investigations

- Learns to apply the full process of technological design, combined with relevant science concepts, to solve problems
- Learns how energy and matter interact, how the water cycle functions, and how inherited variations can become adaptations to a changing environment

Grade 8

WRITING

- Writes for a variety of audiences and purposes, including persuading and explaining
- Analyzes ideas, selects a manageable topic and elaborates using specific, relevant details and/or examples
- Knows and applies spelling, punctuation, capitalization, grammar and paragraphing appropriate to the grade level

READING

- Integrates a variety of comprehension and vocabulary strategies and adapts reading to different types of text
- Summarizes information from multiple sources to deepen understanding of the content in oral and written responses
- Continues to read for pleasure as understanding of author's craft deepens

MATH

- Knows and applies the properties of integer exponents
- Solves equations with one variable and pairs of equations with two variables
- Compares graphs, equations, tables, and verbal descriptions of functions

- Uses graphs, equations and tables to represent real-world situations and solve problems

SCIENCE

- Learns to think critically and logically to make connections between prior science knowledge and evidence produced from their investigations
- Learns to apply the full process of technological design, combined with relevant science concepts, to solve problems
- Learns how energy and matter interact, how the water cycle functions and how inherited variations can become adaptations to a changing environment

Grade 9

WRITING

- Writes for a variety of audiences and purposes, including persuading and explaining
- Analyzes ideas, selects a manageable topic and elaborates using specific, relevant details and/or examples
- Knows and applies spelling, punctuation, capitalization, grammar and paragraphing appropriate to the grade level

READING

- Shows awareness of vocabulary and comprehension strategies used, especially when encountering difficult text and/or reading for a specific purpose
- Shows greater ability to make connections and adjust understandings as knowledge is gained
- Continues to increase academic vocabulary

MATH (ALGEBRA I)

- Uses functions to model various situations and solve problems
- Solves a variety of equations and inequalities, understands solving equations as a process of reasoning and explains the reasoning
- Uses equations, graphs, expressions and other algebraic representations to model real-world and mathematical situations using correct math language, terms and symbols

SCIENCE

- Learns to construct sophisticated system models, including the concepts of subsystems, boundaries, flows and feedbacks
- Extends and refines understanding of the nature of inquiry and ability to formulate questions, propose hypotheses and design, conduct and report on investigations
- Develops an understanding of forces, the formation of the universe, and how organisms participate in the cycles of matter and flow of energy to survive and reproduce

Grade 10

WRITING

- Writes for a variety of audiences and purposes, including persuading and explaining
- Analyzes ideas, selects a manageable topic and elaborates using specific, relevant details and/or examples
- Knows and applies spelling, punctuation, capitalization, grammar and paragraphing appropriate to the grade level

READING

- Shows awareness of vocabulary and comprehension strategies used, especially when encountering difficult text and/or reading for a specific purpose
- Shows greater ability to make connections and adjust understandings as knowledge is gained
- Continues to increase academic vocabulary

MATH (GEOMETRY)

- Formalizes geometrical experiences from earlier grades and uses more precise definitions in developing proofs
- Develops the concepts of congruence and similarity and applies right triangle trigonometry
- Connects algebraic formulas to geometric concepts in order to analyze, model and solve real-world problems

SCIENCE

- Learns to construct sophisticated system models, including the concepts of subsystems, boundaries, flows and feedbacks
- Extends and refines understanding of the nature of inquiry and ability to formulate questions, propose hypotheses and design, conduct and report on investigations
- Learns that cells have complex molecules and structure that enable them to carry out life functions such as photosynthesis and respiration and pass on their characteristics to future generations

7

SMOOTH MOVES:

From One School Level to the Next

Getting Ready for School is a detailed checklist for parents who are preparing to send their child to kindergarten. It's full of great suggestions for parents and caregivers with activity ideas, cultural considerations, lists of needed skills, and other valuable concepts all written from the perspective of a kindergarten-bound child. **THE FOUNDATION FOR EARLY LEARNING** created this checklist after holding dialogues with over 300 parents in Washington State. And while its aimed at parents of pre-school children, it also contains timeless advice on behavior, culture, and social interactions that are applicable to kids of all ages.

—Marc Sachnoff, Chief Parent, The Parents Union

GETTING YOUR PRESCHOOLER READY FOR SCHOOL

excerpted from the brochure "Getting School Ready," www.gettingschoolready.org)

What do children need to be ready for kindergarten? If children could tell us, here's what they might say: **I need to get along with others.**

You can:

- Show me ways to make new friends.
- Help me understand how I can be friends with children who are different from me.
- Teach me what to do when someone hurts my feelings.

I need to know how to talk with others and to listen.

You can:
- Talk with me about things I'm interested in.
- Teach me how to know when it's my turn to speak and when I need to listen.
- Teach me words to describe my feelings and needs, and when to use them.

I need to feel excited and comfortable about starting kindergarten.

You can:
- Let me know you're excited about me starting kindergarten.
- Give me a chance to visit my school before I start.
- Listen to my thoughts and ideas about school.
- Play a game with me to pretend I'm in school already.

I need to know what kindergarten will be like.

You can:
- Teach me to follow directions by giving me simple steps.
- Help me learn how to share with other children, stand in line, wait my turn, and sit in a circle.

I need to feel good about myself.

You can:
- Pay attention to me and listen to my ideas.
- Help me feel good about all the things I can do.
- Praise me for my strengths.
- Be patient and let me develop at my own pace.
- Teach me that all my feelings are okay, but not all my

actions are okay. For example, it's okay to be upset, but it's not okay to hit others.

- Teach me ways to calm myself down when I get frustrated.

I need to feel good about my family and culture, and to learn about other cultures.

You can:

- Show me books and pictures of people who look like me.
- Show me books and pictures of people from other cultures.
- Sing songs and tell me stories from my culture and from other cultures.
- Use the language(s) I know to help me understand and learn.
- Take me to places that teach me about my culture and other cultures.

I need to be excited about learning.

You can:

- Encourage me to explore with my senses—to see, touch, smell, hear and taste my world.
- Give me fun, exciting choices.
- Give me lots of time to figure things out.

I need to learn to try things and keep trying even when it seems hard.

You can:

- Give me activities that hold my interest.
- Help me explore and try new activities.
- Help me learn step by step.

- Teach me that making mistakes is part of learning.
- Show me different ways to understand my world.

I need many ways to express myself.

You can:

- Help me dance, sing, whistle, play instruments, paint, draw, color, build, invent, and make believe.
- Help me care about others and help them, too.
- Help me notice and talk about flowers, trees, animals, clouds, the sky and water.

I need to be familiar with words and books.

You can:

- Teach me new words.
- Show me words and symbols in my language and the sounds they make.
- Read to me. Take me to the library. Bring me books and magazines.
- Ask me questions about stories to help me understand their meaning.
- Sing songs and teach me rhymes.

I need to know shapes, sizes and colors.

You can:

- Give me things to sort by shape, size and color.
- Help me find and name shapes and colors all around me.

I need to learn to count and understand that numbers have meaning.

You can:

- Help me play counting games.
- Let me count things at home and in my community.
- Show me how numbers are used around me.

I need to be safe and feel safe.

You can:

- Help me practice saying my name, address and phone number in my home language and in English.
- Teach me about watching for cars and not talking to strangers.
- Teach me who to ask for help when I need it.

I need to have bathroom and self-help skills.

You can:

- Teach me the words to tell other grown-ups when I need to go to the bathroom, or when I am feeling sick or hurt.
- Help me practice going to the bathroom, washing my hands, dressing, and tying my shoes.
- Encourage me to try things I've learned before I ask my teacher for help.

I need to be able to use my hands and fingers to do small tasks.

You can:

- Help me learn to pick up, hold and use pencils, crayons, markers, paintbrushes and scissors.
- Help me make things with blocks, paper, cardboard and tape.

I need you to help me feel ready and eager, even if I also feel scared.

You can:

- Make sure we both have time to think and talk about our feelings. Your ideas and feelings shape mine. I need you to show me confidence. This is a big step for our family!
- Help me practice saying goodbye to you so I can get ready to join the school group easily. Kindergarten is different than preschool or childcare where parents might stay with a child for some time until they feel ready to say goodbye. Help me learn to be on my own with my teacher and fellow students.
- Be delighted to see me after my day at school! Be ready to ask specific questions about what we did that day and who my new friends are.

I need good food, rest, and play to have the energy to learn.

You can:

- Make sure I get enough rest every night, even if I don't want to go to sleep. I can't learn if I am grumpy and tired at school.
- Give me healthy food every day, especially breakfast.
- Ask for a form for free and reduced breakfast and lunch if our family needs help getting me the healthy food I need.
- Make sure I have time and safe places to play. Kids need at least one hour of exercise each day. Outdoor play is very important for me!

HOW TO ENROLL AND WHAT TO EXPECT ABOUT ME

My name is _____

My parents/guardians name(s) are _____

_____

My address is _____

_____

My phone number is _____

My school district is _____

My school is _____

My school address and phone number are _____

_____

_____

My teacher's name is _____

I'm excited about school because _____

_____

My questions about school are these _____

_____

My local library is _____

I need you to let the school know that I am coming.

You can:

- Call and visit my school the year before I start. Each school district has its own rules, so it is important to talk to them.

- Visit my teacher and describe what I know and can do.
- Share things happening in my life that affect how I feel and act.
- Find out about any special needs I have.
- Learn about our family's rights in the school.
- Learn about school and community services we might need, especially if we speak a language other than English.

I need you to know what the school expects from me and my family.

You can:

- Meet with my teacher to see what he or she expects me to know and be able to do. School has changed since you went!
- Get an up-to-date list of my immunizations.
- Find out what information my school needs about me and when they need it. My school might need a copy of my birth certificate, immunization record, or proof of address.
- Find out when teachers set aside time to meet with parents. If those times don't work, let me know what times do work.
- Ask the teachers what kind of help they expect me to get from my family at home.
- Volunteer to help at my school.

RESOURCES

- For school readiness news, resources, and information about the history of this project visit the Foundation for Early Learning at www.earlylearning.org and click on *Getting School Ready!*

- Visit nces.ed.gov/globallocator to find your child's school information.

- Research Washington state schools at reportcard.ospi.k12.wa.us.

- Call the WithinReach hotline at 1.800.322.2588 or visit www.parenthelp123.org for family health information and referrals.

- Ask your librarian for books, music, videos, and other resources. Libraries also have programs, such as story times, that can help your child prepare for school.

- Printed guides are available in Cambodian, Chinese, English, Korean, Russian, Somali, Spanish, Tagalog, and Vietnamese. To download print-ready pdf files, visit earlylearning.org/gettingschoolready. To purchase booklets, contact the Foundation for Early Learning at info@earlylearning.org or 206.525.4801.

ERIN JONES is the equity and achievement director for Federal Way Public Schools, one of the most diverse school districts in Washington state. In this piece, Erin lays out very specific steps that parents can take to help their elementary school student make the important and sometimes difficult transition to middle school. As a former teacher, the mother of three teenagers and a former assistant superintendant of schools for the state, she brings a well-rounded perspective that is based on her own experience.

—Marc Sachnoff, Chief Parent, The Parents Union

PREPARING FOR YOUR STUDENT'S SUCCESS IN MIDDLE SCHOOL

BY ERIN JONES

The transition from elementary school to middle school or junior high is one of the most critical transitions in a young student's life. Middle school/junior high students do not typically drop out, but they can become disconnected. This phase of life is typically difficult for both students and parents (puberty is not easy!), but it can be a fun time, if you are prepared, patient, and supportive. Here are some recommendations for you from a mother of three teenagers and a former middle school teacher. See www.k12.wa.us/CISL/ for other resources related to supporting your student in public education.

1. **Establish clear, consistent routines and expectations.** In

elementary school, students typically have one teacher with one set of expectations for the entire day. That is not the case in middle school or junior high. Students may have up to six different teachers with six different sets of expectations. Although students at this age tend to push back on rules, they are doing so for security—they need to know there are still boundaries and that they are safe. The more you can create a consistent environment at home, the better off your student will be in all areas of his or her life. Here are some ideas:

- **Homework:** Make sure your student does some homework every night at the same time, so it becomes habit. Even when there is no homework, have work available for your student to do or encourage him/her to write in a journal.

- **Reading:** Make sure your student reads at least 30 minutes every night.

- **Dinner:** Do your best to eat dinner together as often as possible, and use the opportunity to talk to your student about how school is going.

- **Grades:** Let your student know what your expectations are for grades—positive reinforcement is often more effective than punishment (for example, offer an incentive for students who hold a certain grade point average or for students who improve grades from one quarter/semester to the next). Although grades do not follow students into high school, the habits and practices that lead to those grades do follow students.

- **Bedtime:** Set a daily bedtime and stick to it! Students should be getting eight to ten hours of sleep each night in order to grow and maintain health.

■ **Media:** Monitor the amount of TV and technology your student watches daily. Have conversations about what is watched and played—teach your student to be a critical thinker about all the media to which he or she is exposed.

2. **Make sure your student is taking the most rigorous courses available to him/her.** Not every student is at the same level. Some students have learning disabilities, some are gifted, some are in the process of learning English, some have unique learning styles. Make sure you have spoken with your student's teachers to determine which courses and support will be most appropriate. If you believe your student has been placed in the wrong courses, ASK QUESTIONS! Do not assume the school is always right. Sometimes students are accidentally placed in the wrong courses, or the school may be unaware of your student's needs. Here are some things to consider:

■ **Math:** Math courses taken in middle school can drive whether or not a student can get the right courses to attend a four-year college or university, so make sure your student is correctly placed.

■ **Second language:** Learning a second language is easier at a younger age. Students should begin to take world languages as soon as they are available.

■ **Getting help:** If students are behind in a skill, NOW is the time to get help. Do not wait until high school.

3. **Make sure your student participates in at least one extracurricular activity.** Students need a place to belong. Students who feel like they belong are more likely to perform well academically and develop strong self-esteem.

Here are some ideas:

- **Variety:** Encourage your student to try a variety of activities—from sports to arts to social clubs—as many students are just learning about their interests and talents.

- **Budget:** Many extracurricular activities are free, but if there is a fee and you are unable to pay, ask the school for help. Schools generally have a fund to help with this.

4. **Make early and regular contact with your student's teachers.** Many teachers will reach out to you within the first month of school, but if they don't, reach out to them. They need to know you are on board and interested in partnering. Here are some things to share with them:

- **Strengths/areas of growth:** Teachers will get a list of students needing special support, but often they do not have time in the first month to look carefully at that list, so be specific about your child's needs.

- **Interests:** Let your child's teachers know about any particular interests she/he has outside of school—sports or instruments played, cultural clubs, etc. This can help the teacher choose relevant reading material and make special connections with and for your student.

- **Special family circumstances:** The following events or situations could impact the way a student performs or interacts with others: divorce/separation, siblings, adoption, a recent move, a death in the family.

- **Communication:** Find out how each teacher would prefer to communicate when there is a concern or a question—face-to-face meeting, phone call, text message, or email. Include the times that are best for you, and don't be ashamed if you are not available during the school day. Teachers are often not available at that time for their own children either.

5. **Make sure your student participates in academic activities during the summer months.** Students can lose up to a year's worth of learning over the course of a summer if they are not engaged in academic activities. Here are some ideas:

   ▪ **Activity ideas:** Look to your school district, the Boys and Girls Club, the YMCA, and your local parks and recreation department for free or low-cost summer activities.

   ▪ **Reading:** Encourage your student to continue reading 30 minutes at least five days a week during the summer.

   ▪ **Workbooks:** Purchase a grade-level workbook for your student to work through (check Costco, Barnes and Noble, Half-Price Books, a teacher supply store, and even Goodwill).

   ▪ **Field trips:** Take trips to local museums, monuments, concerts, and colleges/universities (it's never too early!).

6. **Take time to celebrate successes with your child.** Middle school students often feel like they don't measure up—academically, socially, physically. Take time to celebrate even the smallest improvement. Success breeds success. Be sure to attend all special events in which your student is participating—concerts, sporting events, and other celebrations. Middle school/junior high students often say they don't want you around. However, they do appreciate your presence (even from a distance).

7. **Apply for the *College Bound* Scholarship.** Not all students will qualify for this scholarship, but many will. See http://www.wsac.wa.gov/PreparingForCollege/CollegeBound for more information about eligibility. Students and families must apply for the scholarship by the end of 8th grade to qualify. For families who do not qualify, please set aside money now, if you have not already. You could even encourage your student to begin to put aside his/her own money (even in small amounts) from allowances or birthday gifts to invest in their future education.

BEV FALGIONE is a psychologist who has worked with groups and clients as diverse as inner city high school boys and suburban real estate brokers. She has a keen eye for unspoken discomfort and upset that kids may be holding in. And very few kids are really ready to make the big jump from Elementary to Middle School. The anxiety and confusion can really impact our kids' ability to function at their best. In this piece, Bev provides you with an array of check lists, online parent and child preparation tests, and other resources to help you help your child get off to a good start in Middle School.

—Marc Sachnoff, Chief Parent, The Parents Union

TRANSITIONING FROM ELEMENTARY TO MIDDLE SCHOOL

BY BEV FALGIONE

Panic, fear, excitement are all to be expected as your child leaves elementary school behind and embarks on a new journey into the world of increased responsibility and independence in middle school.

It's only natural for both you and your child to have concerns about entering an academic setting with multiple teachers, multiple classrooms, more limiting teacher accessibility, reporting changes, and mounting volumes of homework. This transition chapter is intended to provide you, as the parent/guardian, with practical guidelines, checklists, and resources to support your child through his or her academic rite of passage.

Children learn some very valuable lessons during this time of growing. Personal relationship challenges will often seem to take priority over schoolwork, and communication with your child will be critical. There will be times when you have to let your child solve her or his own problems, and other times when you have to step up as the voice of authority. Boundaries still need to be identified as part of understanding the responsibilities that come with increased independence.

There will be times that a "no" from you will provide the very out that your child needs to avoid a situation that he or she is not prepared to manage alone.

Keep the communication going between you and your child. *Scholastic* has produced (with the help and guidance of Barbara J. Murray, M.A., school counselor for the Morris Plains, N.J., school district) two quizzes, one for parents, one for children. Click on the link below to take the quizzes, and then use the answers to open nonjudgmental discussions with your child.

The Results page at the end of each quiz will identify your parenting style, and your child's action style, giving you clues that can make the transition an exciting experience.

Click here: www.scholastic.com/familymatters/ parentguides/middleschool/quiz_situations/index.htm

Remember that your child needs your support, and keep in mind that pushing you away is a normal part of adolescence. What he or she really wants and needs is for you to stay involved.

You and your child both have fears about transitioning into middle school. Let's compare the three top fears of parents vs. the three top fears of children transitioning from elementary to middle school:

Parents/Guardian

1) Will my child fit in, make friends, or give in to peer pressure?
2) Is my child properly prepared socially and academically?

3) Will my child be safe going to, from, and while at school?

Children
1) Will I fit in and have friends?
2) Will I be able to locate my locker and remember the combination to the lock?
3) Will I be able to locate the restrooms, classrooms, and remember my schedule?

The following checklists will begin to break down those fears with knowledge. The checklists do not represent every item to be considered. Rather, they are a starting point for you to customize for your specific child's needs.

Checklist: Setting the Stage for Transition
Parent/Guardian and Child Together
- Geographically locate school
- Determine best and safest transportation to and from school
- Map out route to and from school
- Indentify emergency alternative route
- Establish safety rules and code word
- Identify emergency contacts, numbers, and prepare a list

Checklist: Parent Orientation
Review with Child
- Review school policies, specifically
  - ✓ Dress code
  - ✓ Social media
  - ✓ Cell phones
  - ✓ Bullying
- Attendance and tardiness
  - ✓ Schedule and required testing during the school year

✓ Standardized state testing

✓ Homework expectations

✓ Student/parent dashboard for homework assignments and communications

✓ Lines of communication with teachers (note: middle school teachers typically have infrequent communications with parents unless there are behavior issues, so parents need to initiate dialogue and set the expectations for scheduled communications.)

✓ Role of school counselors and procedure for communication

Checklist: Physical Tour of the School

- Places and Things to Locate During Walking Tour
- Parent and Child Together

✓ Classrooms

✓ Restrooms

✓ Lockers and practice lock combination at home

✓ Counselor's office

✓ Main office

✓ Gym

✓ Phone for students' emergency use

✓ Emergency exits

Checklist: Setting the Stage for Good Study Habits
Parent and Child Together

✓ Designate specific, consistent space for homework

✓ Establish study time schedule

✓ Use a homework journal

✓ Review homework with child

✓ Use a separate pocket folder for each subject

✓ Engage the services of a tutor or enroll in after-school tutoring program

Checklist: Ways for Parents to Stay Engaged

- Volunteer at School
  - ✓ Explore ways you can have a presence if not during school hours, perhaps after hours or evenings as your work/personal schedule permits
  - ✓ Interaction with school staff in a more social atmosphere can potentially give you more insight into the classroom
- Attend open houses
- Meet as many of the other parents as possible
- Join parents/school organizations

Examples of neutral/positive hypothetical questions that can build your child's confidence about being prepared for middle school:

- If you finish your work early in class, what are some good things to do until the class ends? (e.g., do homework for another class, read, draw, rest quietly)
- If you were to have trouble with a classmate and were feeling frustrated, what might you do? (e.g., talk to my teacher, talk to the school counselor, walk away)
- You rushed out the door to school and forgot your lunch. What would you do? (e.g., go to the office and call, ask for a credit on my hot lunch account)
- Spend time with your child to create as many questions as possible.

Remember that transitioning from elementary school to middle school is a natural rite of passage for your child. As a parent, embrace it by being present.

RESOURCES:

www.scholastic.com

http://school.familyeducation.com

www.stopthedrama.org

www.stompoutbuying.org

www.education.com

www.pbskids.org

www.findingdulcinea.com/guides/Education/Middle-School-Math.html
   (middle school math resource)

www.homeworkspot.com

If you thought making the big move from elementary school to middle school was challenging, wait until you try to help your middle school student transition to high school. In middle school, your child has a lot more room to make mistakes, miss assignments, and even fail a class. Not so in high school, where everything stays on his or her transcript and counts toward widening or narrowing college options. **ERIN JONES**, equity and achievement director for Federal Way Public Schools, lays out specific steps that you can take to help your student make a successful move to high school. As a former teacher, the mother of three teenagers, and a former assistant superintendant of schools for Washington state, she brings a well-rounded perspective that is based on her own experience.

—Marc Sachnoff, Chief Parent, The Parents Union

THE TRANSITION TO HIGH SCHOOL

Everything that is true for the transition to middle school or junior high school is the same as the transition into high school. Students and staff will tend to suggest that there is not as great a need to be connected with your student in high school as you were in middle school or junior high. This is not true, although the connection may look different. Continue to have consistent expectations and routines. Although you need to begin to loosen the reigns a bit over time, as your student proves him/herself to be responsible, you still need to have clear expectations. Continue to be visible and accessible. Your student may not want to talk every day but will want a listening ear when necessary. Remain in close contact with your student's teachers and keep a close eye on your student's grades via the online grade book (there are many different kinds—see your school district's website for details). Continue to promote participation in extra-curricular activities during the school year and throughout the summer months.

There are two critical items that are different about this transition from the one into middle school/junior high: graduation requirements and preparation for college.

1. **Graduation requirements**: Although there are general state graduation requirements (see http://www.k12.wa.us GraduationRequirements/default.aspx), school districts often have their own, which can be found on the district website. Make sure you are aware of those requirements and that your student is registered for the number and type of classes needed to graduate on time. Do not hesitate to contact your student's counselor if you have questions or concerns. Most schools have either online classes or summer school available for students who get behind due to illness or to failing a class.

2. **Preparing for college:** Although many school districts have graduation requirements that align with college entrance requirements, that is not true everywhere. Please see http://www.wsac.wa.gov/sites/default/files/Revised MCASOverviewParents-April2011_1.pdf for information about the course requirements for attendance at a college/university in Washington state. Make sure to check your student's transcript at the end of each year to make sure your student is on course not only to graduate but to be eligible to attend a college/university if he or she chooses. Also make sure you are talking about your student's interests and exposing him/her to local community colleges, technical colleges, four-year colleges, and universities

early (you do NOT have to be a college graduate to talk with your student about education after high school). There will be college fairs at your student's high school. Find out when they are and plan to attend as early as your child's sophomore year. Finally, as your student enters his/her junior year, make plans to visit any institutions that are of interest to your student. Looking at school brochures or websites never gives a complete picture of a community. It is also important for admission officers to meet your student face to face, so your student will be more memorable come application time (anywhere from fall to spring of senior year). Scholarships are available for college, but they will take time to find and complete. Every school counseling center will have scholarship information. Start soon and ask teachers for letters of recommendation weeks in advance of due dates. See http://www.wsac wa.gov/PreparingForCollege/CollegeBound for more information about preparing for college.

8

WHAT IS GREAT TEACHING?

There's a lot of debate going on in the world of education these days about the best ways to prepare students for college and career. The old ways that you and I may have been taught may no longer be as effective in helping our kids get ready for 21st century jobs that might not even exist today. **DR. WILLARD DAGGETT**, the founder of the International Center for Leadership in Education, has been proposing a new way of looking at the teacher-student relationship and the function of modern public education. The piece he contributed, while not directly aimed at parents, will give you a quick understanding of the paradigm shift going on in hearts and minds of innovative educators. But for a quick summary, take a look at the chart at the end of the piece. If you're like me you'll see a lot of the education you got in the "Traditional" column. And you may want to ask your school principal or district super-intendant just how committed they are to moving your kid's education towards the ideas listed in the "What Is Needed" column.
Interesting reading…

—Marc Sachnoff, Chief Parent, The Parents Union

CONVERGING CHALLENGES

The following is excerpted from The Daggett System for
Effective Instruction—Where Research and Best Practices Meet

WILLARD R. DAGGETT, CEO

International Center for Leadership in Education

While our schools are working hard at improving, the reality is that the rest of the world is changing faster, leaving a growing gap. In an effort to close the gap, state-supported initiatives for raising standards and measuring student achievement will require schools to change what and how they teach. The "fewer, clearer, higher" Common Core State Standards (CCSS), anchored by the "next generation assessments" (NGA), will raise the bar for most states to help ensure that every student is challenged to achieve and succeed. Proficiency levels will be set higher. Assessment will measure not just what students know, but also what they can do with that knowledge. Most schools involved with Race to the Top (RttT) initiatives will need awareness building, planning, time, and support to realize the mandatory 2014–2015 implementation dates of the new learning expectations represented by the CCSS and NGA.

These challenges are driving a greater focus on accountability and a growing demand for proof of effectiveness and efficiency in public education. If No Child Left Behind's Adequate Yearly Progress (AYP) provision laid accountability for results on the backs of principals, today's education policy, including measures such as growth models and teacher effectiveness evaluations, is shifting the burden of accountability to teachers.

WHAT WORKS — ANALYSIS OF THE RESEARCH

Recognizing the challenges facing schools today is easy. Identifying the most effective ways to address them is not. Education research is plentiful and comprehensive, so much so that studies are available to prove or disprove almost any decision made by education leadership. However, most of the respected research is consistent on one key school improvement issue: effective instruction really matters. No single variable has more impact than teaching. …

IT TAKES A SYSTEM, NOT JUST A TEACHER

Research supports what most of us see as common sense: what goes on between the teacher and the each student is central to high-level learning. Effective teaching is not the end goal, however; it is the means to an end: student achievement.

Nevertheless, all teaching is more effective when effectively supported. Achieving the goal of improving instruction requires a supportive and aligned system. Stated another way, although effective teaching is essential, it is not sufficient to maximize achievement for all students. This understanding of the need for an organization-wide commitment is at the heart of the Daggett System.

Daggett System for Effective Instruction

For decades, the International Center has been an active observer of and participant in education reform. The International Center's "on the ground" work with schools has reinforced that it takes an entire system to develop, maintain, and enhance effective instruction. Teachers must be supported by instructional leadership and organizational leadership.

The Daggett System has been significantly informed by:

1. **Observing and disseminating best practices**. ...
2. **Current and past research**. ... At the same time, the Daggett System departs from some of the existing models and frameworks for teaching in several significant ways.

Traditional Teaching Frameworks	Daggett System for Effective Instruction
What teachers should do	What the entire system should do
Teacher-focused	Student-focused
Teachers deliver instruction	Teachers facilitate learning
Vision is set by top leaders	Vision is built more inclusively
Define vision primarily in terms of academic measures	Define vision as strong academics and personal skills and the ability to apply them

Rigid structures support adult needs	Flexible structures support student needs
Focus on teaching	Focus on learning

The Daggett System leverages more than the teacher in the classroom. It emphasizes vertical alignment—with organizational systems and structures and with instructional leadership—and horizontal alignment—with teaching colleagues and classroom resources—as keys to success. Because teachers are the most powerful influence on instruction, the entire system needs to be focused on making teachers effective. Therefore, the Daggett System provides a coherent focus across an entire education system: Organizational Leadership, Instructional Leadership, and Teaching.

ORGANIZATIONAL LEADERSHIP

Organizational leadership is a function, not just a person. It involves a mentality, structure, focus, and commitment to create the environment in which learning is optimized. Six primary functions of Organizational Leadership are listed below.

Create a culture of high expectations. That culture must communicate and encompass:

- *Why*: the challenges of changing demographics, a wired and tech-savvy generation of students growing up in a digital world; as well as a global economy in which America must innovate and compete.

- *To Whom*: students, staff, and community stakeholders.

- *How*: through active and ongoing communications and

messaging at staff development events, community forums, business roundtables, and so on.

Create a shared vision. Culture needs to be embedded in goals and action plans focused on instructional effectiveness that all stakeholders can understand, contribute to, and commit to. ...

Build leadership capacity. Organizational leadership needs to enhance existing leaders and identify and cultivate the development of emerging, future leaders. ...

Align organizational structures and systems to vision. Once culture, mission, and distributed and empowered leadership are established, Organization Leadership needs to

- decide which external impediments to instructional effectiveness can be changed or compensated for and which are beyond the control of the education organization

- ensure enabling conditions and structures to support instructional effectiveness are in place

- identify which factors impacting effective instruction are most effective and efficient ...

Align teacher/administrator selection, support, and evaluation. Organizational Leadership's role is to adopt "talent management" systems for recruitment, retention, development, and evaluation that are understood, broad-based, focused on instructional effectiveness, and aligned horizontally and vertically among all individuals who support instructional effectiveness and student achievement. ...

Support decision making with data systems. Organizational Leadership needs to ensure that a data system is used to inform and enhance instructional effectiveness. …

INSTRUCTIONAL LEADERSHIP

Instructional Leadership is directly focused on instructional effectiveness and ultimately student achievement. Instructional Leadership can be provided by a variety of people, functions, and means in support of teachers, such as:

- district and regional instructional leadership
- principals, assistant principals
- department chairs
- expert teachers, counselors, social workers
- mentor teachers, teacher coaches, teaching peers/team leaders.

The Instructional Leadership segment of the Daggett System concentrates on five overarching elements:

Use research to establish urgency for higher expectations. The first job of Instructional Leadership is to reinforce the vision set forth by Organizational Leadership. …

Align curriculum to standards. Instructional leaders also need to prepare teachers for the new types of instruction and formative assessment. …

Integrate literacy and math across all content areas. Literacy and math are essential for success in college and careers.

Facilitate data driven decision making to inform instruction. To meet the needs of diverse learners, teachers must use data to measure student growth and inform and differentiate instruction. …

Provide opportunities for focused professional collaboration and growth. [Research] clearly shows the importance of teacher selection and development, and a continuous cycle of evaluation and support. …

TEACHING

If Organizational Leadership does its job to establish an overarching vision and mission, deal with obstacles, align systems and build leadership capacity; and if Instructional Leadership ensures that tools, data, and support are made available and accessible to teachers; then the vanguard of instructional effectiveness—teaching—will be well supported in addressing the daunting challenges of the classroom.

Drawing on the research on teacher effectiveness and observations of best practices for two decades, the Daggett System includes the following six broad elements under Teaching.

Embrace rigorous and relevant expectations for all students. Teachers must embrace the organizational vision that all students can and will learn and must strive to help every student reach his or her fullest potential. This is the attitude that effective teachers bring to class every day. Embracing high expectations is an offshoot of commitment and caring for individual students. …

Build strong relationship with students. … The presence of strong, positive, trusting relationships impacts student engagement and therefore fuels students' sense of belong-ing and commitment to their own learning. ...

Possess depth of content knowledge and make it relevant to students. While teachers must have strong content expertise in the subjects they teach, effective instruction is more than just a transmittal of knowledge. It is equally the ability to make connections, show relevance, nurture engagement and embed understanding. ...

Facilitate rigorous and relevant instruction based on how students learn. Every teacher needs a thorough understanding of pedagogy as well as a versatile and comprehensive repertoire of instructional strategies—classic and innovative—to draw from in planning and providing instruction so they can match teaching approaches with learning objectives, subject matter, and targeted learners.

Teachers also need a clear understanding of today's students who are "wired differently"; who want to see a reason for learning something; who fascinate their elders with their technology skills—in fact, they take connectivity and instant access to information and to one another for granted; who multitask; and, perhaps most significantly, who would rather "do to learn" instead of "learn to do." They collaborate naturally and seamlessly. Not surprisingly, they simply learn differently. The abundance of recent discoveries in neuropsychology and brain research can and should inform teachers' understanding of 21st century learners.

Demonstrate expertise in use of instructional strategies, technology, and best practices. Teachers must become comfortable and skillful in "wherever learning" strategies. In successful schools, learning takes place in the classroom, by completing an individual assignment, working in groups, sitting with a tutor, learning online, via cell phones, smart boards or using a computer, completing a family lesson around the kitchen table, in a lab, in the gym or band room, at an outdoor education center, at a museum, on a field trip, and interviewing a guest speaker. Instructional effectiveness extends far beyond the walls of the classroom. ...

Use assessments to guide and differentiate instruction. Good teachers always ask themselves: "Did they ALL get it? How do I know they got it? How do I measure mastery? How do I help those students who didn't? How do I know at any given point in the year if students are on track to achieve?"...

SUMMARY

The Daggett System for Effective Instruction is more than an approach to enhancing instruction and instructional capacity. It is a way of thinking about what we believe about children, schools, and learning which has coalesced at a critical time in American education when standards, assessments, accountability, teacher evaluation systems are intersecting with budgets, the global economy, technological innovation, "wired kids," and public policy debates.

The Daggett System builds upon the ideas, inspirations, practices, and research of others, including the best research and meta-analysis on effective instruction and the years of collective experience that International Center staff, consultants, and thought-leaders have accumulated and harvested from thousands of American schools. The Daggett System recognizes the primacy and immeasurable value of great teachers and great teaching and strives to align education systems and functions with what teachers need to be the best support to learners. It does so by looking not only at teachers, but also beyond the classroom to inspire leadership at all levels in support of instruction. The Daggett System challenges all educators to consider the possible with a sense of practical urgency and a buoyant sense of the possible.

The Daggett System for Effective Instruction is a way to transform a traditional system into one that better supports all teachers and more fully prepares every student for college, careers and citizenship.

TEACHERS	
TRADITIONAL	**WHAT IS NEEDED**
"Deliver" instruction	"Facilitate" learning
Student	Learner
Test scores (easy to measure)	Holistic assessment of learner (difficult to measure)
Proficiency	Growth
Standardized approach	Personalized, differentiated for each learner
Content-focused and narrow (Quadrants A/C)	Application focused (Quadrants B/D) Probing questions, scaffolding
Instruction in classroom only, bell schedule-limited	Learning any place/anytime, 24x7, technology
Teacher-centered	Learner-centered
Passive learning	Active learning
Learn to do	Do to learn
Assessment has single purpose (proficiency)	Smarter, balanced assessments with multiple purposes (assess for proficiency, growth, formative, predictive)
Teacher as "sage on the stage"	Teacher as facilitator of learning

Define learning in terms of required content to teach	Define learning in terms of skills and knowledge as results
Define learning from specific skills up to total student	Define learning from whole student down to specific skills
Cover as many topics as possible	Help students learn priority skills deeply
Break apart curriculum	Integrate curriculum
Entire curriculum mandatory	Curriculum includes some student choice
Teach skills in isolation	Teach skills in context
Focus on deficiencies	Focus on proficiencies
Look for evidence of good teaching	Look for evidence of good learning
Standardized procedures	Shared best practices
Give separate assessments	Give embedded assessments
Isolate instruction from community	Connect instruction to community

INSTRUCTIONAL LEADERS	
TRADITIONAL	**WHAT IS NEEDED**
Manage in the current system	Change the system
Use past experience to solve problems	Learn new ways to adapt and change
Promote standard procedures	Adapt to unique situations
Replicate practices with fidelity	Create new practices to meet student needs
Look to supervisors for answers	Look to staff to take actions
Rely on individual expertise	Share each other's expertise
Authority	Collaboration

ORGANIZATIONAL LEADERSHIP	
TRADITIONAL	**WHAT IS NEEDED**
Set vision by top leadership	Set vision with wide contributions
Define vision in few academic measures	Define vision in term of whole student needs (LC)
Place priority on short term results	Place priority on long•term improvement
Limit goals to best students	Expand goals to all students
See vision as top leaders' initiative	Embrace vision universally
Instill fear with goals	Inspire passion with goals
Rigid structures to support adult needs	Flexible structure to support student needs
Top down change for ease of administration / compliance—teachers as objects of change	Top down support for bottom-up reform—teachers as agents of change

REFERENCES

Hattie's paper Influences on Student Learning:
www.arts.auckland.ac.nz/staff/index.cfm?P=5049

The Sutton Trust Toolkit of Strategies to Improve Learning, Durham University:
www.suttontrust.com/public/documents/toolkit-summary-final-r-2-.pdf

Marzano: www.marzanoresearch.com/documents/RacetotheTopWhitepaper_Marzano.pdf

InTASC Model Core Teaching Standards: A Resource for State Dialogue:
www.wresa.org/Pbl/The%20INTASC%20Standards%20overheads.htm

Charlotte Danielson's The Framework for Teaching, The Danielson Group at
www.danielsongroup.org/theframeteach.htm

Sutton Trust Toolkit of Strategies to Improve Learning:
www.suttontrust.com/public/documents/toolkit-summary-final-r-2-.pdf

The American Recovery and Reinvestment Act, U.S. Department of Education:
http://www2.ed.gov/policy/gen/leg/recovery/presentation/arra.pdf

International Center for Leadership in Education 1587 Route 146 • Rexford, New York 12148
518-399-2776 • www.LeaderEd.com

The days when parents could just drop off their kids at school and expect the teachers to "smart 'em up" are long gone. We need to know the quality of instruction each of our children is receiving. And every child deserves a great teacher. But how do we, as parents, recognize great teaching? Teach for America Fellow, Kipp School veteran and public middle school math teacher **CHRIS EIDE** gives you a good place to start.

—Marc Sachnoff, Chief Parent, The Parents Union

WHAT DOES GREAT TEACHING LOOK LIKE?

BY CHRIS EIDE

Teachers are leaders, and in each classroom a movement is afoot. The most effective movements are those that have a clearly defined and ambitious goal, where all of those in the movement are motivated toward that goal, and where the path to that goal is clear. In an effective classroom, you will tend to see evidence of a great movement.

But what does it look like?

Many people are led to believe that great teachers have large, charismatic personalities who entertain and enlighten students in a marvelous act. There may be some great teachers who can be described in such a way, but others aren't. For a moment, think back to the teachers who taught you the most. It might not be the larger-than-life character you had in mind. In many cases, the teacher who taught you the most was the one who made you work hard, who may have even seemed mean by the amount of time they demanded you spend on your studies.

A great teacher has built relationships with his students and understands what conditions he needs to create in his classroom so that all of his students will succeed. He understands that each student interacts with others in particular ways and by careful orchestration. He can create a symphony out of a classroom of young people. Great teaching is indeed an art, but there are several elements that are at the core of the practice of most all great teachers.

THERE IS A GOAL

Like any strong leader, a teacher has a goal for what he wants his class to achieve. The goal must be motivational for everyone involved and yet reachable through hard work. If the goal is reached, the outcome will benefit not just the individuals in the class, but also the entire class and even inspire those who will come after. Legendary calculus teacher Jaime Escalante (who was lionized in the film *Stand and Deliver;* for more information, see "Resources" below) had a simple goal: to get his students at a traditionally failing high school in East Los Angeles to pass the AP calculus exam. They all knew the goal, and when they reached it, growing numbers of students who followed were able to reach that goal because they had seen what is possible.

When you enter a classroom, you should be able to ask students and the teacher what the goal for the year is, and they should all be able to tell you.

THERE IS A PLAN TO GET THERE

A goal is empty without a plan to get there. The plan must be adaptable, but it must always keep the goal in mind. In a classroom, this means that the teacher will have laid out benchmarks throughout the year to determine whether his students are on track. This often takes the form of midterm assessments of some kind. His lessons will be designed so that when students meet the lesson objectives, the benchmarks for success will be met. A great teacher will take accountability when students have not met the mark, because he will have been the one who designed and executed the lessons. This is increasingly being anticipated using techniques such as "exit tickets," which are short (2–3 questions) assessments given to students at the end of each class or class segment, which the teacher will use to determine whether the students are ready to move to the next lesson. It will also help inform the teacher about which students need more time with the given subject matter. More often, teachers are using daily data and assessments to help inform their teaching so that they can more accurately reach all of their students.

When you enter a classroom, you should see the teacher collecting and using data to inform their plan for how to reach their goal. Their benchmarks for success should also be clear and aligned to their goal.

EVERYONE IS INVOLVED

A learning classroom may be loud and it may be pin-drop silent, but regardless of the sound, all of the students know what is expected of them and are working hard to get to that standard. The teacher is never content and always demands more—neater writing, clearer thinking, elaboration, new solutions. A teacher who is content with any student's progress has set the bar lower than it could have been. Regardless of whether a student has special needs, a great teacher will hold that student to a high level of expectation for growth. No student should feel like it is all right to take it easy and coast.

When you enter the classroom, you should see examples of what excellence looks like, examples of growth and evidence that progress is being made toward the goal.

WHAT TO LOOK FOR IN A CLASSROOM

- A clear goal that is motivational for all students, posted on the wall.

- All students able to recite the goal.

- A daily lesson that clearly leads to the goal (if the goal is for students to pass the state test, for example, the daily lesson should align to the state's learning standards).

- Methods of data collection (exit tickets, classroom "clickers," daily quizes) that inform the teacher on the daily progress of students.

- Clear examples of the level of expectation for student work, effort, and behavior posted on the walls.

RESOURCES

- If you want to see a great teacher in action, take a look at Raif Esquith in the Los Angeles Public Schools: www.cbsnews.com/video/watch/?id=2419428n http://youtu.be/ddqhFhSe7bw
- Esquith, Raif, Teach Like Your Hair's On Fire: The Methods and Madness Inside Room 56 (New York: Viking Adult, 2007).
- For more about Jaime Escalante, check out http://youtu.be/IM6blsMhPRQ

Great teachers motivate their students to master the material they are studying by engaging them in a compelling and relevant learning experience. In order to understand what kind of classroom experience your child is having its useful to know what an optimal learning experience might look like in which the students are highly motivated to work in collaboration with each other and the teacher – because they love what they are doing! In this piece **DR. MARGERY GINSBERG**, director of the Leadership for Learning Program at the University of Washington, presents a model for student engagement and motivation with four basic conditions that work together to support a natural interest in learning.

—Marc Sachnoff, Chief Parent, The Parents Union

A LITTLE MORE ABOUT MOTIVATION

THE MOTIVATIONAL FRAMEWORK FOR CULTURALLY RESPONSIVE TEACHING

(from *Transformative Professional Learning*, by Margery Ginsberg, pp. 144–146)

All human beings are motivated. However, not all human beings are motivated to learn what a teacher may want them to learn. *The Motivational Framework for Culturally Responsive Teaching* (Ginsberg, 2011) provides a coherent set of research-based teaching practices that work together to support students' *will* as well as skill as a learner. It helps educators plan and improve instruction so that they can create compelling and democratic learning experiences that honor the diverse perspectives, values, and talents that students bring to the classroom.

The motivational framework has four basic motivational conditions that support students' natural interest in learning:

(1) "Establishing Inclusion" reminds teachers to create learning environments where students feel connected to and respected by peers and their teacher. Because this condition is essential, teachers often make a home visit to develop a relationship with a child's entire family.

(2) "Developing a Positive Attitude toward Learning" reminds teachers to offer students choices and opportunities to learn in ways that are not only relevant to attaining a good grade, but that are relevant to students' strengths and values. Because this condition is essential, teachers often help students set personal goals before they embark on a new learning experience.

(3) "Enhancing Meaning" reminds teachers to create learning experiences that challenge and engage each and every student. Because this condition is essential, teachers challenge students' thinking with questions that go beyond mere facts and require students to apply or analyze what they know.

(4) "Engendering Competence" reminds teachers that students need authentic evidence of their effectiveness, and well as a hopeful orientation to achieving success. Because this condition is essential teachers give students opportunities to *show*, as well as write about what they have learned. Also teachers give students opportunities to resubmit their work until it meets a high standard of achievement.

Parents and family members can apply these same criteria to (1) family interactions, (2) homework support, (3) "look-for's" when visiting their child's classroom to see how it is supporting their child's learning needs.

OVERVIEW OF THE MOTIVATIONAL FRAMEWORK FOR CULTURALLY RESPONSIVE TEACHING

The Motivational Framework for Culturally Responsive Teaching provides a *macrocultural* pedagogical model. It is built upon principles and structures that are meaningful within and across cultures, especially with students from families that have not historically experienced success in school systems. It does not compare and contrast groups of people from a micro-cultural perspective, one that, for example, identifies a specific ethnic group and prescribes approaches to teaching according to pre-sumed characteristics and orientations.

The purpose of the motivational framework is to unify teaching practices that elicit the intrinsic motivation of all learners so that educators can consistently design learning experiences that matter to and support the success of all students. Therefore we have sought to make the framework broad enough that it accommodates the range of ethnic and cultural diversity found in most schools. It also integrates the variety of assumptions addressed in many disciplines—educational, political, social, and psychological. In terms of everyday instruction, it seeks to explain how to create compelling and democratic learning experiences that honor the diverse perspectives, values, and talents that students bring to the classroom.

Four Conditions of the Motivational Framework

The motivational framework offers a holistic representation of four basic conditions (i.e., attributes in a learning environment) that work together to support a natural interest in learning:

1. Establishing Inclusion
2. Developing a Positive Attitude
3. Enhancing Meaning
4. Engendering Competence

Establishing Inclusion refers to principles and practices that contribute to a learning environment in which students and teachers feel respected by and connected to one another. It is the core of genuine empowerment and agency. As human beings we seldom accept high levels of personal challenge unless there is a sense of emotional safety. If a person is to grapple with uncertainty and dissent, the learning environment must welcome the worth and expression of each person's true self. For this to occur there need to be norms, procedures, and structures that contribute a sense of support and unity. Examples of this include communication agreements or ground rules and collaborative learning that promotes genuine opportunity for all people to contribute.

Developing a Positive Attitude refers to principles and practices that contribute, through personal and cultural relevance and through choice, to a favorable disposition toward learning. This means that learning is contextualized within the students' experience and is accessible to them. It also means that students are encouraged to make real choices based on their experiences, values, strengths, and needs. It has been said that, generally, jurors make up their minds within the first 10 minutes of a trial, after which it is most difficult to influence their opinions. Students are in a parallel situation. Who among us will feel positively about learning when information and ways of defining talent exclude one's own experiences and strengths? Examples of this motivational condition include personalized goal setting and approaches to accessing prior knowledge such as KWL (know-want to know-learn).

Enhancing Meaning refers to challenging and engaging learning. It expands and strengthens learning in ways that matter to students and that have social merit. This condition focuses on substantive learning experiences. It is intellectually rigorous in ways that involve higher-order thinking and critical inquiry. Examples of this motivational condition are inquiry-oriented projects, role-playing and problem solving, and case study analysis.

Engendering Competence refers to principles and practices that help students authentically identify what they know and can do and that link students to a sense of hope. This motivational condition includes rubrics that are created with students to clarify what success looks like, demonstrations of learning connected to students' frames of reference, self-assessment, and grading practices that encourage learning.

The four conditions work *in concert* to encourage and support the intrinsic motivation of a broad range of students, within and across cultural groups. Intrinsic motivation supports higher levels of cognition as well as the notion of lifelong learning (Deci & Ryan, 1991; Ginsberg & Wlodkowski, 2009; McCombs & Whistler, 1997). Unfortunately, in many schools, especially those that serve low-income populations, there tends to be a strong reliance on extrinsic rewards. In such instances, it is not uncommon for students to be rewarded or punished for behavior related to learning that lacks relevance and challenge. Strong schools know that no single teaching strategy will consistently engage all learners, but they also recognize that a repertoire of random strategies can be equally ineffective.

Pedagogical randomness can create motivational contradictions such as cooperative learning combined with competitive assessment, or project-based learning without the "emotional safety" for risk taking and inventiveness. While some students are prepared to endure school under just about any circumstances, an increasing number of students are not. This is especially true of students who are neither implicitly nor explicitly connected to a hopeful future. For them, school achievement does not promise impressive credentials, jobs, or income (Fordham & Ogbu, 1986).

While the motivational framework includes strategies for each condition, it also serves as a template for recognizing existing strengths in educational practice and providing clues to develop those strengths. In this way, it is respectful of the work that educators are already doing while it encourages classroom teachers to apply principles of motivation for all students with constancy.

9

WHAT DOES A GREAT SCHOOL LOOK LIKE?

Generally, when I ask parents about the quality of their children's school, they will answer, "Uh, I think it's pretty good." When I probe a little deeper, the hesitation I hear comes from the lack of any real understanding that most of us as parents have about what actually makes a school great. How do we determine the quality of our children's schools? There are various sites purporting to provide such data, but frankly the only way to really know is to visit your child's school. And what should you be looking for? Teacher **CHRIS EIDE** shares some great places to start in this piece.

—Marc Sachnoff, Chief Parent, The Parents Union

WHAT DOES A GREAT SCHOOL LOOK LIKE?

BY CHRIS EIDE

I t is important to note at the beginning of this short chapter that it is nearly impossible to tell whether a school is great simply from its appearance. I have seen powerful instruction and school leadership in a school located in a strip mall and I have seen unfocused teaching and vacant school leadership in elegant buildings that look like royal mansions. The appearance of a school is not always an indicator of its greatness. The greatness of a school lies within its walls, be they made of brick and mortar, carbon fiber or cardboard. So, when the question "what does a great school look like?" is asked, we have to get past the exterior to meet the people inside.

In my first year of teaching, in search of inspiration, I was advised to go visit a school across town. When I arrived, the students were transitioning between classes and as I walked up to the main entrance, the door opened up for me. It was an eighth grade girl who had noticed a visitor to her school approaching the door, broken away from her group of friends and gotten to the door before I did. "Welcome to our school. Can I help you find somebody?" she asked. I was stunned. I challenge you to find an eighth grade person who will walk away from their friends to engage in conversation with someone they don't know and then offer to help. Most *adults* wouldn't do that. I barely knew what to say. "Yes, I'm looking for the school director," I managed and she brightly replied, "right this way!" Just as I was about to ask whether she had been planted there to open the door for unsuspecting visitors, she asked, "So what are you reading?" Just by contrast, I had come from a school where earlier in the day, I had said 'hello' to a student at my school and they had looked at me up and down before turning to spit on the closest locker. The difference was obvious. As a first year teacher, I was buried in books designed to help me get better. I had nothing elegant to offer her. "I'm reading a book on psychology as applied to teaching," I said to her, and she frowned. "No. Fiction! What fiction are you reading?" It fully occurred to me then that I was totally outclassed by an eighth grader who just happened to be passing by at this school. I confessed to her that I wasn't actually reading any fiction at that time when she left me with her lesson for the day: "That's too bad; you should always be reading a work of fiction. Here is the director's office, I hope you have a nice day."

To be clear, it isn't that a passing student happened to change my expectations for what is possible inside of three minutes that made that school great. She was simply a signal that perhaps that school was likely to have motivated students who were proud to be there. I saw what truly made that school great when I visited classrooms, met with the school director, and spoke with more students. The school had defined a mission and was very clear about how they were going to achieve their goals. The goal of this school was to make sure that 100% of their students either met or exceeded grade-level expectations, no matter what, and that they formulate ideas on where they will go to college. The school leader was constantly in classrooms, providing creative feedback so that each student and teacher would continue to improve. Teachers and students knew that they had to improve in order to meet their goal, the goal that classes before them had nearly all met. In this school, whose population is low-income and minority students, the quest for academic perfection defines the culture.

CULTURE WILL TELL YOU ABOUT THE SCHOOL'S RECENT HISTORY.

This had created a school culture focused on academics that in turn made students proud to be there, proud to know that they were a part of something that would give them more opportunities in their lives, proud to introduce complete strangers to their school. You should be able to read a school's culture within the first 30 minutes of being inside a school.

Look around; are students moving with a purpose, generally toward their next class? Are there signs of recent success such as posters showing academic progress, college pennants or extracurricular victories? Listen for a second; is the school quiet when it should be quiet and loud when there is a purpose to the loudness? Also, what does the school 'feel' like? Do you feel that the people in the building have a general sense of urgency? Are adults in the hallway during passing periods, urging students to be on time to class with inspirational words? In classrooms, are the teachers vigilantly on top of what the students are doing, guiding and redirecting? Are students actively engaged in class and purposeful and positive in their actions?

All of these are signs that the adults have worked hard to create a positive, focused and urgent culture at their school, and that the students have largely if not entirely bought into that culture. Creating that culture is a highly intentional and difficult thing to do.

Details are very important.

When a teacher at the school that I visited found a piece of gum under one of the seats, the school director taped an excerpt from "The Tipping Point" by Malcolm Gladwell to every student's locker. The excerpt was an outline of "The Broken Windows Theory" that says that one broken window in a neighborhood leads people to think that it's okay to break window there. Soon, all the windows might be broken. In the case at the school, when one piece of gum is allowed under a seat, the school could easily become a much less beautiful place that people aren't as proud of. In many schools around the country, you could find a piece of gum under a seat, but at this school, even that much needed to be addressed. Details are very important. That school community values respect for their environment and when the director brings even the smallest details forward as a big deal, students and teachers are reminded that every little thing in their work matters too.

In general, if members of the school community are focusing on small things like gum under the seat, it is a sign that the bigger issues are all under control. If students are thinking about gum under the seat and seeing much that matters for their school community, writing on desks, walls, graffiti or other vandalism issues are out of the question and a violation of the school culture.

Students can help you find out what you need to know.

Not all students in a great school will be like the one who opened the door for me as I entered the school that day. In fact, many students in great schools won't be entirely forthcoming with praise for their school during the course of a school day. This is because they are working hard and people who are in the midst of important deadlines aren't often friendly or conversational.

Students in not-so-great schools are also likely to complain, but for different reasons. Complaints like "we have to do too much work" are much better than "the kids here are out of control."

Complaints like "we never get to play" or "the teachers here are mean" require more investigation. Sometimes, students who are in need of strong academic support will feel as though they are being bombarded with work and will complain that they don't get to play enough. If the school's goal is to get every student to grade level academic expectations, that student might actually be asked to study longer than her peers, not as a punishment but to give her a better opportunity to succeed in class. Some students also confuse teachers demanding a lot of work from their students as being mean to them.

In general, complaints that use extreme language ("always," "never," "crazy," etc.) require more investigation. If you have access to students who have graduated from your child's school 1-3 years in the past, they will be very reliable sources of information because they will have been able to contrast their recent school experience against their experience at your child's school. Often times, students who felt that they had to work too hard at a school are able to see the value of that hard work in their new school environment. They are more likely to be appreciative of those teachers who were demanding on them, giving you a more accurate picture of what each teacher's strengths are.

What to look for at your child's school:

- A clear mission for the school and intense focus on details related to the mission.

- Signs of recent successes that will raise the level of expectation for current students (for example: "82% last year's 8th graders passed the state science test"; "the girls' ultimate Frisbee team placed 2nd at the regional tournament," etc.).

- People (adults and students) acting positively and with purpose.

- Focused and intentional instruction in every classroom (see Chapter 9 for more details).

- School leadership that is present and active in improving the performance of students and teachers.

Equity is a hot topic in education these days. Parents want their own children to get a great education and we also want all kids to get a great education. But with the impact of budget cutbacks, the politicizing of school decisions, and a disparaging large set of achievement gaps between white and Asian students and many of their Hispanic, African-American and Native American schoolmates, equity has become an important issue. **ERIN JONES** is the Equity and Achievement Director for Federal Way Public Schools, one of the most diverse school districts in Washington State. In this piece Erin explains the difference between equity and equality and provides a clear list of ways that schools should be addressing equity issues.

And if you discover that your school is lacking in one or more of these elements, in addition to contacting the Governor's Ombudsman for Education (the official Washington State advocate for parents), later chapters in this book will provide you with tools for advocacy and action to make change.

—Marc Sachnoff, Chief Parents, The Parents Union

SO, WHAT DOES *EQUITY* HAVE TO DO WITH IT?

BY ERIN JONES

What is *equity* anyway? According to *The American Heritage® Dictionary of the English Language,* equity is *the state, quality, or ideal of being just, impartial, and fair,* OR *something that is just, impartial, and fair.* Equity is NOT necessarily equal. Equity does not mean that each student gets the same thing. Students come to school with a variety of experiences, needs, resources, and support. Schools and districts with an equity focus do their best to ensure that each student, no matter what he or she brings to the table, has access to the same opportunities and gets to "play the game of school" on a level playing field.

What does this mean for you and your student in the public education system? There are a variety of ways equity should play a role at the district level, although that will need to be addressed in a later article. Here are some things to consider as you look for equity in your student's school:

1. **In a school that practices equity, you and your student will see your culture and the culture of your community expressed.**
   - You will see yourselves and all others who live in your community represented in pictures on the walls of the hallways and classrooms.
   - You will see books in the library and in classrooms written by, about and for the variety of students represented in your building.
   - Your school will have expectations (for academics and behavior) that align with the values, traditions and practices of the diverse students represented in your building.
   - Your student will experience teaching strategies/styles that are relevant to the many diverse experiences of the students in your building.
   - You will see staff and community volunteers who represent the cultural backgrounds of the students served in your building.
   - You will see staff who recognize difference and/or diversity as an asset to your community.

2. **In a school where equity is practiced, the school will communicate with all families clearly and regularly.**

- Your school will communicate important information in the languages that are spoken by the families in the school community.
- Your school will provide interpreters at school events for families who do not speak English fluently.
- Your school will avoid using academic/complicated language that is only understood by teachers and others who have a background in public education.
- Your school will communicate in multiple ways - via email, notes home, face-to-face, and phone calls - to accommodate the needs of all families.
- Communication, especially related to decision-making, will involve opportunities for families and students to provide feedback to staff at the school.

3. **In a school where equity is practiced, your student will be able to take the classes that best match his/her abilities and potential.**
   - You will see each student placed in the classes that best suit his/her needs. Students who have particular learning challenges will receive the support they need, and students who need more challenging curriculum will be provided with opportunities to work at a faster pace.
   - You will see special education classes, highly capable classes, and all other special programs mirror the ethnic and socioeconomic backgrounds, as well as the gender breakdowns of the student population.
   - You will see all students challenged with rigorous curriculum but also provided with the support necessary to be successful.
   - You will see staff who have high expectations for each and every student.

- You will see staff who are clear about the options that are available for students and communicate clearly about why students are selected for particular course loads and how students and families can change a course or courses, if they so choose.
- You will experience clear communication between the school and each student, beginning in middle school/junior high, about the path to college or university.
- You will see master scheduling driven by what's best for students.

4. **In a school where equity is practiced, consequences for behavior are the same for all students.**
   - You will see students and families involved in the development of classroom and building expectations.
   - You will see all staff members in a building implementing expectations in the same ways.
   - You will see expectations and consequences for student behavior that are clearly communicated to both students and families.
   - You will see students acknowledged/rewarded in similar ways for "good" behavior.
   - You will see students experience fair and impartial consequences for "bad" behavior.
   - You will see administrators and staff who communicate clearly and immediately with family and students the reason(s) for consequences, particularly if those reasons involve removing a student from the classroom or building for any period of time.
   - You will see discipline data that shows discipline referrals proportional to the numbers of students of a particular gender or ethnic group in the building.

When you see inequitable practice in your school building or district, speak up. Always assume best-intent first (assume that a teacher or school is trying to do the right thing but may be misguided). It is never a good idea to make assumptions without hearing all sides. Don't hesitate to ask for a meeting with a teacher or principal. Bring a friend with you who can be a support and take notes. If the practice or policy is hurting students or families and you do not feel your concerns have been heard, see if your district has a family engagement director or coordinator or a director of equity. They can often assist as facilitators or mediators. If there is no such person, contact an *education ombudsman*, who can help you advocate (toll free number: 1-866-297-2597).

Many of us simply don't know what's going on inside our local school building. We bring our kids to the door or to the bus stop, but other than the semi-annual parent-teacher conference or the occasional Halloween Carnival, we really don't have much of sense of whether our school is great, good, so-so, or poor. And that just won't cut it for most of us anymore.

We need to be able to determine the quality of instruction, learning and attention to each child's needs that are taking place beyond the big doors. In their *Picky Parent Guide*, **DR. BRYAN AND EMILY HASSEL** have identified seven Great School Quality Factors that can help you begin to understand how your school ranks beyond test scores and opaque awards. And they provide you with six key questions to ask the principal — and what you should hear from them — to determine whether they are really leading towards achieving those seven Great School Quality Factors or not.

And if they're not, it's time to either create a plan of action to revitalize the school leadership, change it, or change schools.

—Marc Sachnoff, Chief Parent, The Parents Union

THE SEVEN GREAT SCHOOL QUALITY FACTORS

(from *Picky Parent Guide: Choose Your Child's School with Confidence*, by Bryan C. Hassel, Ph.D., and Emily Ayscue Hassel, pp. 182–184)

Fit matters, but quality counts, too. We define high quality or "great" schools as ones in which students of all kinds learn dramatically more in core academic subjects than similar students in other schools. That's what Great Schools accomplish. Great Schools meet the needs of more children and families more of the time. The results show both in "soft" measures, like parent satisfaction, and "hard" ones, like student test scores in the basics. [You can] look for the signs of a Great School, one that you can count on to educate your child in core academics, year in and year out.

But what are Great Schools made of? Sugar and spice and everything nice? Snips and snails and puppy dog tails? Wouldn't it be nice if you could relay on simple clichés for raising your child and choosing a school? But parents of spunky girls and good-as-gold boys know that what seems true at a glance doesn't always hold true.

So how do you find these Great Schools? What's the magic ingredient to seek on the label so that you know you're getting real quality? Test scores, individual teacher quality and other parents' opinions are frequent misleading indicators.

- **Test scores** alone reveal little unless you know whether you are comparing schools with similar kinds of students: ones of simiar starting capabilities or from families with similar parent education levels and incomes.

- **Great teachers** are, well, great. But absent a Great School behind them, they are less likely to stay and spread their good work to other classrooms. Like all stars, they are likely to "burn out" over time without a fuel source for their challenging work. And you never know whether your child will be assigned to more than one or two star teachers over the years.

- **Your friends' glowing reports** of their own children's school experiences mean little unless your friends know about the real indicators of school quality, have fit needs similar to your child's and family's, and know about more than their own children's particular teachers.

Fortunately, decades of research by many different experts of differing perspectives have shown that a few consistent features of schools make them great. Not just for your one child—but for all of your children, and for the kids on the other side of the railroad tracks, too. Not just for today, but for tomorrow and the next year, too.

We call these consistent features the *Great School Quality Factors.* When compared to typical schools, Great Schools consistently demonstrate these seven pillars of school quality:

1. **Clear Mission Guiding School Activities:** The school has a clear purpose and approach to education that *you* understand. The principal, teachers and parents understand this mission, and it guides all decisions and activities in the school. Precious resources like money and classroom time are focused to achieve the school's goals, not wasted on "window dressing"—things that may look good but don't further the school's mission.

2. **High Expectations for All Students:**

   The school has *high* minimum academic standards ("grade level") that prepare *all children* for independent adulthood in our society. Grade level standards may include both specific skills and knowledge a child should have in core subjects, as well as "thinking" skills. In a Great School, all students are expected to achieve at least grade level.

   The school also has higher, individualized standards for children who are ready to excel beyond grade level. No matter how bright the average child in a school and how high "grade level" goals are set, every school has students who are ready to learn beyond these goals. In Great Schools, these students are expected to meet increasingly difficult goals in core subjects.

3. **Monitoring of Progress and Adjusting Teaching.** Each child's individual progress is monitored frequently during the school year. Teachers change their teaching approaches as needed—adapting to individual student interests, learning styles and other differences—to ensure that students meet their goals, both grade level and higher. When a child falls behind, the school takes immediate action, accepting no excuses for failure.

4. **Focus on Effective Learning Tasks.** Teachers use well-planned, well-tested approaches to instruction. Class time, material purchases and facilities are all allocated according to the school's mission; more important subjects are given more time and the best materials and facilities. Classroom interruptions are minimal. Materials and curriculum are frequently reviewed, and altered, to ensure they are working as planned.

5. **Home-School Connection.** Parents are told what their children will be learning, how to help at home, how their children are progressing during the year (frequently), and how to work with the school to solve any problems their children might face.

6. **Safe and Orderly Environment.** Students are kept safe from harm by other people, facilities and equipment. Students know how they are expected to behave in and out of the classroom, and they behave as expected because consequences are clear and consistent.

7. **Strong Instructional Leadership.** School leaders maintain clear, high expectations for teachers, recruit and keep great teachers, organize teachers to work together, monitor and improve teacher performance, and act on high and low

teacher performance (ridding school of low performers, recognizing and rewarding high performers).

If you've already had a child in school, you may find yourself saying, "I knew it!" to several of the seven Great School Quality Factors. They each affect real, tangible activities in the classroom that you and your child cherish when they're present and sorely miss when a school is lacking.

ASSESSING SCHOOL LEADERSHIP: TAKE THE LEAP

(from *Picky Parent Guide: Choose Your Child's School with Confidence*,
by Bryan C. Hassel, Ph.D., and Emily Ayscue Hassel, pp. 240–243)

Even with a narrow focus on *instructional* leadership, many parents feel uncomfortable evaluating the leadership of a school from afar, and indeed it is easier once you've had more contact with a school as parent of a current student. But there's no reason not to take a stab at it as you investigate schools. Often a school's top leader will jump out at you as "just the thing" or "way off." But sometimes it is hard for parents to put into words and feel confident about their impressions of a principal or other school leader. Nonetheless, you will see the result of those leadership strengths and weaknesses as you look at other Great School Quality Factors.

Fortunately for you, there are simple signs that a school's instructional leadership is strong or weak. If you have limited time or are just taking an initial look, probe your targeted schools on questions 1 and 6.

1. IF YOU ASK THIS...

Do you have clear expectations of teachers in your school?

You should hear this...
- We have clear, written goals and expectations for all staff
- All goals and expectations for staff were chosen to support our school's mission and quality
- We also expect certain behaviors from teachers when interacting with students, parents, and other staff, and they are...(fill in blank)

- We use these overall goals and behavior expectations to determine each teacher's development and improvement goals every year

Not this…
- Each teacher decides what's important in her class
- All of our teachers are great–they have a lot of experience
- Our teachers are professionals and can figure out what they need to do (true they are professionals, but all professionals in an organization need clear expectations)

2. IF YOU ASK THIS…

How do you get and keep great teachers?

You should hear this…
- We recruit for skills, competence and previous performance, not just years of teaching experience
- We recruit people who have already shown that they can meet the expectations we have of current teachers, in teaching or similar pursuits
- We would rather leave a position temporarily unfilled than bring in a teacher we're not sure about
- We don't let the district send us teachers who won't work well here
- Our best teachers stay because they are valued and rewarded
- Top teaching candidates want to teach here, because they know their work will be valued and rewarded
- We work hard to keep our current staff improving, and both our good and great teachers like this

Not this...
- We've tried but haven't had much luck
- We take who we can get and figure it out after they get here
- We recruit teachers with the most experience only
- The district assigns teachers to our school

3. IF YOU ASK THIS...

Do teachers work together in your school?

You should hear this...
- We have time set aside weekly for staff in the same grades and subjects to evaluate student progress, identify problems and plan changes together
- Everybody has strengths, and we expect staff to work together to make the most of their strengths
- Our best performers coach or model their work for our other teachers

Not this...
- When we have time
- We have a weekly all-school staff meeting for announcements
- Our teachers meet to chat and support each other personally, which they love (fine if they do, but not a school quality indicator!)
- Our teachers are professionals and can do what they want in their own classrooms

4. IF YOU ASK THIS...

What does your school do to help teachers improve their teaching?

You should hear this...

Most Important:
- We monitor individual teachers' strengths and challenges, and we start there to improve
- Teacher improvement is focused on better meeting our school's mission
- Teacher improvement is focused where student performance isn't meeting the school mission
- Teacher improvement is an everyday activity, not just for teacher workdays
- I observe teachers and give feedback about both strengths and challenges

And Also:
- I work with each teacher to develop both strengths and weaknesses
- Teachers observe each other and give feedback
- Teachers "coach" each other
- Development activities vary – workshops, training programs, independent study – but all focus on what teachers need to meet our mission

Not this...
- Teachers focus their development mainly on areas of personal interest
- Our teachers are professionals and they take care of their own development

- We hire only the best and so do not need to worry
- Teachers figure this out for themselves; they don't need help
- Our teachers attend conferences and workshops (fine, but only in combination with other efforts and only if workshops chosen to improve skills related to mission)
- Teaching is a natural talent; some people have it, and some don't

5. IF YOU ASK THIS...

Do you reward your high-performing teachers?

You should hear this...
- We reward our high-performing teachers in many ways, such as:

  • Recognizing their performance publicly
  • Paying for them to attend conferences
  • Providing extra funds for special projects
  • Increased pay (e.g., annual bonus pay or higher salaries)

Not this...
- We provide the same rewards to all teachers, regardless of performance and regardless of how that makes our best performers feel about the school
- We don't want to embarrass our solid performers by recognizing our best performers
- You can't really tell who the best performers are

6. IF YOU ASK THIS...

What do you do if a teacher is not performing up to expectations?

You should hear this...
- We quickly focus on the areas that the teacher needs to improve and help her develop. If this does not work, the-teacher is asked to leave our school (e.g., no more than 90 days from time problem is detected).
- We do not allow teachers who don't meet the school's performance expectations to stay
- While we respect our employees personally, the education they provide to students is our #1 concern

Not this...
- We give teachers a few years to figure this out
- We are a public school, so we cannot get rid of low performing teachers
- We never have low performers
- It is too hard to find replacements, so we just don't let people go
- Employee job security is our #1 concern

10

HOW TO FIND THE BEST SCHOOL FOR YOUR CHILD

At The Parents Union we often get asked "what is the right school for my child?" There isn't a simple answer, but the materials in this book should help you begin to sort through all the elements that you might want to consider in making this important decision. Long past is the day when you could just drop you kid off at the local school door step and tell them – as my uncle did – to "smart 'em up." Instead we as parents first need to understand our goals for each of our children. We also need to understand what their learning styles are, and then we can begin to assess the options available.

Fortunately, a lot of the hard work has been done by **DR BRYAN AND EMILY HASSEL** in their excellent book, the *Picky Parent Guide*. In this piece you'll find a simple grid you can use to get started on the process of determining what kind of school is best for each of you kids based on your family needs. And they give a lot of great questions to ask the principal of your local school or other schools you may be considering.

FAMILY NEEDS:

What to Look for In a School

Family Needs: What to Look for in a School

How to Use This Table:
- ➤ Make sure you have identified your family's top needs for school before using this table.
- ➤ For each of your family's Must Haves and Nice to Haves, find the companion section of this table.
- ➤ Read general information about the family need or value where provided.

- ➤ Then read specific information about your family's Must Haves and Nice to Haves.
- ➤ **Bolded** questions and things to seek are the most important. Focusing on them will help you quickly target the best-fit schools and eliminate poor-fit schools.
- ➤ Note top things to seek and ask at schools on your *Personalized Great Fit Checklist* (page 59).

If This is a Must Have or Nice to Have	...Then Look For This in a School	...And Ask These Questions
WHAT YOUR CHILD LEARNS		
Values about what *content* is important ➤ Core academic subjects ➤ Other academic subjects (make your own list) ➤ Morals, ethics, character, religion ➤ Other non-academic: e.g., social, emotional and physical development ➤ Other topics important to you	➤ School clearly states its mission, goals, and curriculum so you know what content will be covered, And: ➤ Includes your valued subject(s) as a stated part of curriculum, including class time devoted exclusively to the subject, or ➤ Includes your valued subject(s) as a stated part of curriculum, and regularly weaves teaching of the subject into other subjects (e.g., science taught as part of math curriculum), or ➤ Includes optional classes or established extracurricular activities in subject, and you are confident child will be able to pursue these opportunities, or ➤ Includes special events, mini-courses, or other non-routine, limited-time exposure to subject	**Principal:** ➤ **Ask specifically about the subjects or topics of interest to you** ➤ **What subjects are covered in the curriculum** (for grades your child will attend at this school)? ➤ Are these taught in separate classes or woven into basic subjects? ➤ **How much time is spent on these subjects** (that are of interest to parent)? ➤ Are there other opportunities – elective courses, mini-courses, extracurricular clubs, etc. – to cover other topics that are not part of regular curriculum? ➤ Are the subjects covered likely to stay the same in the future (especially ones of interest to you)? ➤ What kind of training do teachers have in subjects (most important if math or science is your valued area)? **Teachers:** ➤ What subjects do you cover in your class? ➤ Separately or as part of basics? ➤ How much time do you spend on each subject in a week (ask about subject of concern to you)? ➤ Do you help with any of the other topics covered in mini-courses, clubs, etc? (If so, describe.) **Parents:** ➤ Confirm principal's and teachers' comments ➤ How have your children liked these subjects (of interest to you)? ➤ Is there anything that you think the school should do better in covering these subjects? **Written Materials:** ➤ Look for mention of subject important to you (this indicates that it is a valued and stable part of curriculum) **Observation:** ➤ May want to observe coverage of critical topics in the classroom to ensure that your expectations for what is included are met

Continues...

Family Needs: What to Look for in a School ...cont.

If This is a Must Have or Nice to Have	...Then Look For This in a School	...And Ask These Questions
WHAT YOUR CHILD LEARNS...continued		
Goals for your child: **Grade Progression**	➤ School clearly states that all students are expected to meet grade level requirements ➤ School focuses large portion of school day on basic subjects (reading, writing, math) and any other subjects required for grade progression ➤ School has high percentage of children *like yours* meeting grade level (e.g., percent at grade level for your child's race, family income, previous performance) ➤ School provides individual or small group tutoring for children not meeting grade level requirements ➤ School changes teaching approach if child's progress falls below expected	**Principal:** ➤ Are all children expected to meet grade level, or do you expect that some will fail each year? Why? ➤ What does your school do to help children who are struggling to meet grade level? ➤ How much time in each day is spent on reading, math and writing? Other subjects required for students to pass from grade to grade? ➤ My child is _____ (describe why you think your child may be at risk of not making grade level). What does your school do to help make sure children like that achieve at grade level? **Teachers and Parents:** ➤ Same as principal for each teacher's class **Parents:** ➤ Ask to talk with parents of similar children ➤ Ask how the school has helped their children succeed ➤ Ask what problems they see **Written Materials:** ➤ Look for emphasis on grade level achievement for all **Observation:** ➤ Are teachers engaging all of the children in class: • Making sure that *all* children get a chance to participate and • Making sure that all children are paying attention and • Insisting that all children learn the material?
Goals for your child: **Academic Performance** ...*continues*	➤ School clearly states that it expects children to achieve *beyond* grade level requirements when they are ready ➤ School assesses individual student readiness and sets individual goals, with grade level as a bare minimum; goals are continually raised as child progresses beyond grade level ➤ School monitors children's individual learning frequently (*at least* every 6 weeks, weekly ideal) during year to ensure that unexpected barriers to child's achievement have not arisen ➤ School changes teaching approach if child's progress falls below expected	See Basic Learning Capability section of table *Child Needs: What to Look for in a School*. Ask questions for children of your child's current capability.

Continues...

Family Needs: What to Look for in a School
...cont. — — — A **CONFIDENT CHOICE** Tool

If This is a Must Have or Nice to Have	...Then Look For This in a School	...And Ask These Questions
WHAT YOUR CHILD LEARNS...continued		
Goals for your child: **Academic Performance** ...continued	➤ School does what it should to meet requirements of child with your child's Basic Learning Capability (see *Child Needs: What to Look for in a School*)	See Basic Learning Capability section of table *Child Needs: What to Look for in a School*. Ask questions for children of your child's current capability.
Goals for your child: **College Opportunity**	➤ If child is Challenged or Typical in Basic Learning Capability, choose school for Grade Progression, above ➤ If child is Gifted or Highly Gifted in Basic Learning Capability, choose school for Academic Performance above ➤ For all students: curriculum in elementary should allow entry into middle and high school courses *required* by colleges and universities and *optional* advanced placement level classes in subjects where your child excels	➤ If child is at risk of not passing grade level, see questions above for Grade Progression. ➤ If child may be able to perform beyond grade level, see Basic Learning Capability section of *Child Needs: What to Look for in a School*. Ask questions for children of your child's current capability. **Also ask Principal and Teachers:** ➤ What exactly does your school do to ensure that students in higher elementary grades will be ready to take honors or advanced classes in middle and high school?
HOW YOUR CHILD LEARNS		
Values about school-wide expectations and rules on student conduct: ➤ Manners with other children ➤ Manners with adults ➤ Dress ➤ Discipline ➤ Honor code ➤ Other behaviors	➤ School clearly states its overall values, and ➤ School clearly states its expectations for student conduct both in and out of the classroom, including consequences for not meeting expectations, and ➤ School's rules and expectations for students are consistent with your family's values, including your opinions about these: • Manners with other children • Manners with adults • Dress code • Honor code • General discipline policy (what acts are punished and how punishment is administered) And ➤ School actually adheres to its own values, rules and expectations in daily school life.	**Principal:** ➤ What social values are most important in your school? ➤ Does your school expect certain behaviors and conduct from students in and out of the classroom? ➤ How is that communicated to students and parents? ➤ What are the consequences for not meeting the student conduct expectations? ➤ May want to ask about specific rules and expectations regarding items of particular importance to you: manners expected (e.g., on playground, at lunch), dress code, general discipline policy, honor code. **Teachers:** ➤ Do you find that you are able to enforce your school's conduct rules (be specific: honor code, discipline policy, character code, etc.)? What's the biggest challenge? ➤ What social values do you think are most important in your school? ➤ What kinds of problems do you see with student behavior outside of the classroom, in the lunch room, playground and so forth? ➤ How do students treat other students who are different from the norm?
...continues		

Continues...

205

Family Needs: What to Look for in a School ...cont.

If This is a Must Have or Nice to Have	...Then Look For This in a School	...And Ask These Questions
HOW **YOUR CHILD LEARNS**...*continued*		

Values about school-wide expectations and rules on student conduct:

➤ Manners with other children

➤ Manners with adults

➤ Dress

➤ Discipline

➤ Honor code

➤ Other behaviors

...continued

Parents:

➤ How have you found the social behavior of the other students in your child's school?

➤ Do you like the social values that the school reinforces? Which values? How are they reinforced?

➤ Have you noticed any problems with student social behavior? What? How does school deal with that?

Written Materials:

➤ Look for clear statement of school's social values.

➤ Look for clear statement of student conduct rules and expectations (especially ones important to you).

➤ Look for clear statement of how school expects students to behave in and out of classroom.

Observation:

➤ During your observation time, notice whether teachers insist that children adhere to expected behaviors.

➤ Do teachers treat infractions as mere chances to inflict punishment, or do they use them as a chance to reiterate the underlying values and teach children better ways to behave?

➤ How are students who appear different from others treated?

➤ How do teachers who hear students treating others unkindly respond?

Values about how children should *learn*:

Teaching method

➤ Teacher directed

➤ Student discovery

➤ Mixed approach

Look for clear school statement of teaching methods used throughout the school, and look for method that fits your values.

➤ Teacher directed, look for:
  • Teachers set goals for whole class and define activity steps
  • Teachers, not students, do most of the talking, or teachers direct and control class discussions
  • More whole-class, big-group learning, less small group and individual learning

➤ Student discovery, look for:
  • Students set some individual and group goals within pre-defined topic areas
  • Teachers encourage students to think of questions and discuss or research answers before teachers "tell answer"

Principal:

➤ **Is there a certain teaching method teachers are expected to use here?** Please describe.

➤ Do the teachers decide what activities children will engage in all day or do students have some choice? Is the answer the same for all subjects, or does it vary? Can you give me examples?

➤ Do teachers do most of the talking and directing of discussions? Or are students asked to come up with some of own questions and do some activities on their own? Examples? Vary across subjects?

➤ How much time is spent in whole class, small group and individual activities each day? Does this vary in different classrooms or grades?

...continues

Continues...

Family Needs: What to Look for in a School *...cont.*

If This is a Must Have or Nice to Have	...Then Look For This in a School	...And Ask These Questions
HOW YOUR CHILD LEARNS...continued		
Values about how children should *learn*: **Teaching method** ➤ Teacher directed ➤ Student discovery ➤ Mixed approach *...continued*	• More small group and individual learning, less whole-class, big-group learning	**Teachers:** ➤ Same as principal for each teacher's own class. **Parents:** ➤ Same as principal and teachers – confirm consistency of school's approach. **Written Materials:** ➤ Look for written statement about teaching method expected in school. **Observation:** ➤ Are teachers instructing students in the way described by principal, teachers, parents and written materials?
Values about how children should *learn*: **Classroom behavior management** ➤ Controlling/Strict ➤ Developmental ➤ Mixed approach	**Look for clear school statement of behavior management used** throughout the school's *classrooms*, and look for method that fits your values. ➤ Controlling/Strict, look for: • Clear, written rules of classroom behavior expectations • Clear punishments for breaking rules, rewards for adhering to rules • Little tolerance for not fitting into behavior guidelines ➤ Developmental, look for: • Frequent, small rewards or recognition for positive behaviors • Before exacting punishments, teachers coach students to understand their own emotions (students') and to improve self-control in response to emotions • Teachers modify teaching method to ensure all students are engaged • Teachers use peer group pressure, parents and principal to reinforce expected behaviors	**Principal:** ➤ **Do you expect teachers to take a certain approach to managing children's behavior in the classroom? What approach is expected or commonly used?** ➤ If you do expect a certain approach, do teachers receive any training in this approach? ➤ What does a teacher do if he or she is having trouble managing children's behavior? (Look for principal who acts as coach to teachers, helps them resolve problems and improve behavior management.) **Teachers:** ➤ How do you keep children's behavior in the classroom focused on school work? ➤ What do you do if a child is having behavior problems? **Parents:** ➤ How have you felt about the teachers' handling of classroom behavior? ➤ Have you known about any serious behavior problems among children in the classroom? What do the teachers and principal do about that? **Written Materials:** ➤ Look for mention of how teachers manage classroom behavior. **Observation:** ➤ Does teacher behavior match what you expect based on principal and teacher comments?

Continues...

Family Needs: What to Look for in a School *...cont.*

If This is a *Must Have* or *Nice to Have*	*...Then Look For This in a School*	*...And Ask These Questions*
HOW YOUR CHILD LEARNS...continued		
Your role as advocate for child (understanding, communicating and influencing school to address your child's learning needs). The greater your ability, the less important for school to help you.	➤ School that fits all of your *child's* needs very closely, *or* ➤ School uses individualized approach to student education, including *frequent assessment* of child's academic, social, emotional and physical development. School *changes* child's learning goals and the teaching approach accordingly *And* ➤ **School communicates very frequently with parents about individual children's progress and behavior** (at least weekly is ideal), and ➤ School has very strong and consistent leadership and teacher quality (see Great School Quality Factor #7: Instructional Leadership)	All questions related to your child's specific fit needs, *or:* **Principal:** ➤ How closely are you able to track the individual development (academic, social, emotional and physical) of children at this school? Who is responsible for this? How do they do it? Is it consistently done in all grades? ➤ What changes are made to a child's learning goals and the teaching approach to respond to children's individual needs? ➤ How do teachers communicate with parents about their individual children's progress and behavior? How often? **Teachers:** ➤ Same as principal for teachers' own classes. **Parents:** ➤ Same as principal for parents' own children. ➤ How closely has school monitored your child's development? ➤ How often has school communicated with you about your child's development? ➤ How well has school met your individual child's needs? **Written Materials:** ➤ Look for mention of monitoring children's progress and development not just academically, but also socially, emotionally and physically. ➤ Look for specifics about changing learning goals and teaching approach for individual students. ➤ Look for mention of how teachers are expected to communicate about children with parents.
SOCIAL ISSUES		
Parent Community I want my child's school to have parents with particular characteristics *...continues*	Look for school with parent population that matches the list you have created.	**Principal:** ➤ Ask questions about parent population, according to the profile you have created **Teachers:** ➤ Ask questions about parents each teacher has encountered, according to the ideal list you have created

Continues...

Family Needs: What to Look for in a School ...cont.

If This is a Must Have or Nice to Have	...Then Look For This in a School	...And Ask These Questions
SOCIAL ISSUES...continued		
Parent Community I want my child's school to have parents with particular characteristics *...continued*		**Parents:** ➤ Ask questions about parent population, according to the ideal list you have created ➤ Ask questions of individual parents you meet to see if values and other characteristics are consistent with what you want **Written Materials:** ➤ Look for information about parents that informs you about the characteristics important to you **Observation:** ➤ How do parents speak and act – with their own children, other students, teachers, principal and each other? Does this match what you want? ➤ Do you feel comfortable with other parents from this school? How will your comfort level affect your ability to participate in the school community and help your child build social relationships?
Parent Involvement in School ➤ Helping ➤ Decision-making ➤ Fundraising activities	Look for parent *policy* and *actual* parent involvement that match types and level of involvement you want, including: ➤ Parent Involvement Policy: formal opportunities or requirements for parents to participate in school in ways and at level you want, without obligation to participate in ways or at level undesirable or unfeasible for you ➤ Actual Parent Involvement Level: percentage of parents and time committed actually volunteering at school match what you want ➤ Actual Parent Roles: parents actually participate in school life in ways you want	**Principal:** ➤ **Do you have a parent involvement policy? What is it?** ➤ What opportunities are there for parents to participate in the school? Can you give me examples? (Ask about any specific roles you might want to play.) ➤ Is participation required or optional? ➤ What percentage of parents actually volunteer at the school each year? ➤ How much volunteer time per parent is typical? ➤ Where is most of parent time spent? **Teachers:** ➤ How do parent volunteers help you? Do you find that helpful? Are there other things you wish parents would do to help? **Parents:** ➤ Have you volunteered in the school? What have you done? Was it satisfying? How did it help the school? ➤ What expectations do parents have for each others' involvement? **Written Materials:** ➤ Read parent involvement policy. ➤ In other materials (newsletters, etc.), look for mention of current parent involvement and requests for help from parents – does this match what you want?

Continues...

Family Needs: What to Look for in a School ...cont.

If This is a Must Have or Nice to Have	...Then Look For This in a School	...And Ask These Questions
SOCIAL ISSUES...continued		
Student Community I want my child's school to have students with particular characteristics	Look for school with student population that matches the list you have created.	**Principal:** ➤ Ask questions about student population, according to the profile you have created **Teachers:** ➤ Ask questions about student population each teacher has encountered, according to the profile you have created **Parents:** ➤ Ask questions about student population, according to the profile you have created ➤ Ask questions of individual students you meet to see if behavior and other characteristics are consistent with what you want **Written Materials:** ➤ Look for statistics about student population ➤ Look for mention of student actions and behaviors – do they match what you want in student population? **Observation:** ➤ How do students speak and act – with each other, parents, teachers and principal? Does this match what you want?
I want my child to attend a certain school, school type, or school design	The school, type or design you prefer	➤ If your bias is toward a particular school, confirm that the school has the offerings and characteristics you expected. ➤ If your bias is toward a type of school, confirm that the school has the offerings and characteristics you expect in a school of that type. ➤ If design, confirm that school is in fact using the design as you expect.
PRACTICAL MATTERS		
Child Care ➤ Before school ➤ After school ➤ Holidays ➤ Summer	**School meeting your needs in the following areas:** ➤ Hours and days that care is provided ➤ Transportation to/from school and to/from home ➤ Snacks or meals provided ➤ Safe supervision of child ➤ Academic or developmental assistance ➤ Structured or unstructured time for your child ➤ Care for your multiple children ➤ Cost Stop by your community's child care resource and referral agency for more information about non-school care options.	➤ From any source available to you, find out facts about this school's child care offerings ➤ Ask parents who have used care services about their satisfaction with each aspect important to you (see list to left).

Continues...

Family Needs: What to Look for in a School

If This is a Must Have or Nice to Have	...Then Look For This in a School	...And Ask These Questions
PRACTICAL MATTERS ... *continued*		
Schedule ➤ Daily hours ➤ Yearly (start/finish and holidays)	**Look for school accommodating your daily and annual scheduling needs.** ➤ If available, be sure to look at the coming years, not just the current one, for any changes. ➤ Ask if the schedule is likely to change significantly from year to year	➤ From any source available to you, find out facts about this school's schedule ➤ School web sites and written sources often have the basics of current daily schedule and yearly calendar
Transportation Needs ➤ To school ➤ After school ➤ After school activities	School ➤ Provides transportation or ➤ Is within walking or bicycling distance for you and child (or child alone) to and from home, child care, and extracurricular activities. ➤ Find out what, if any, cost is involved in school-provided transportation	➤ From any source available to you, find out facts about this school's transportation offerings ➤ School web sites and written sources often have the basics of current transportation offerings and cost Parents who have used school transportation: ➤ Have you found school transportation to be reliable (on time, shows up every day)? ➤ Safe (good drivers, good behavior on bus)? If there have been serious behavior problems on the bus, how has the school responded? ➤ Reasonable in cost (if any)? How much?
Location proximity to your home or work	**Look for school in location desired**, near home, work or other critical location	➤ Just note whether location meets your need. May want to rank your school options according to how well they meet your need, e.g., #1= best location, #2 = next best.
Your Other Children	**Same School: Look for school that may be suitable for all of your children** (e.g., that accommodates varying ages and learning needs) **Different Schools: Look for schools with compatible schedules, locations, and transportation** to accommodate your different children without disrupting family life	From whatever source available: ➤ Same School: Determine how well school meets your children's differing individual needs (See Child Needs tables) ➤ Different Schools: Determine schools' schedules, locations, transportation and fit with other family needs to determine compatibility
Money available to pay for school	➤ Schools with combined total cost **(tuition, fees, supplies, dress, lunch, and expected donation, etc.) within your Target (or Maximum)** ➤ Subtract potential scholarship and voucher funds from total cost to determine schools that you could afford	From whatever source available (web sites and written materials are good places to start): ➤ What are tuition and fees for the year? ➤ What other costs should we expect? (Be sure to ask about these: books, supplies, dress/uniforms, lunches, snacks, special fees for trips or other activities, expected donations, class gifts for teachers.) ➤ What scholarships might be available to a child like mine? How do we apply? What are our chances (or how many children get a scholarship like that each year)? ➤ Are government vouchers available that can be used to pay some of tuition here?

11

YOU ARE THE WINNING INGREDIENT IN YOUR CHILD'S EDUCATION

There are lots of things to know in order to help your child succeed in school, and most of them are touched on in this piece by attorney and parent advocate **BETH SIGALL**. I just wish I'd known Beth back when my kids were starting school. She covers so many great points here that can really help you get off on the right foot with your children and their teachers. Working in partnership with educators is always our goal. And together with The Washington Student Success Promise at the end of this chapter, you now have everything you need to know to get started.

—Marc Sachnoff, Chief Parent, The Parents Union

YOU ARE THE WINNING INGREDIENT IN YOUR CHILD'S EDUCATION

BY BETH SIGALL

The starting point for building a successful relationship with your school is to understand how your school thinks about education. A useful way of thinking about it is to understand the concept of macro versus micro. Put simply, macro means having the perspective of the whole or greater good. Micro means looking at something through the prism of a single perspective. The micro framework is an individual, case-by-case analysis. The macro platform looks at the big picture.

When it comes to education, schools, and especially school districts, look at your child from a macro perspective. Parents must view and advocate for their child from a micro perspective.

What does this mean in reality?

Put simply, the "macro" framework means that when a school makes a decision about your child, the school will try to equitably balance the interests of all parties involved—teachers, other students, staff, administrators—and arrive at a decision that considers both the competing and common needs of all those involved. That decision may or may not be what is best for your child.

There is nothing, repeat, nothing wrong with a school considering the greater good in deciding what to do for your child. This is just the reality—it's a value-neutral analysis for the school. Yes, your school wants to help your child, but not in every instance and in every possible way. The school must always consider how helping your child impacts its ability to serve every child. In fact, the school is duty bound to consider how its decisions affect everyone at the school, and sometimes even everyone in the district or the state.

Parents, on the other hand, must function in the micro. *This is because the hard work of parenting can neither be replicated nor delegated, particularly in the arena of education.* Certainly no one endorses selfish disregard for the needs of other students. But the fact remains that at the decision-making table with parents, teachers, and school officials all seated around— parents are the only people in the room whose sole aim is the well-being of their child. **This is the power of parents**.

Parents must understand this basic concept if they want to advocate effectively for their child. They must understand that school decisions are driven by much more than what is best for any single child. It doesn't make the school a bad actor—far from it. The school is trying to their best for *every* child. You are trying to do your best for your child. It is inevitable that at times those missions will have conflicting aims, and you need to understand in those situations the school will at times put your child's interests behind the broader interests. But with this framework in mind, as a parent you'll understand what motivates your child's school and his/her teacher, which in turn will help you understand how to better advocate for your child.

How do I make sure my child is getting personal attention in class?

The key to ensuring that your child is getting personal attention in class is to do these two things:

- Utilize the ready-made opportunities throughout the school year, both formal and informal, for building a strong relationship with your child's teacher

- Develop strong personal and working relationships with other parents at your child's school

Throughout the school year, there are a limited number of formal opportunities for parents to meet their child's teacher and other parents in the class. Because of their infrequency, it's important for parents to attend all of them. If you can't attend, arrange to make up the time with the teacher before or after school on another day.

Here is a typical offering of teacher or school-provided opportunities for parents to connect with their school environment (during the elementary school years).

- Meet the teacher—Many (not all) schools (K–5/6) provide an informal "meet your new teacher" gathering prior to the first day of school (tip: if your school doesn't, consider advocating for one). This setting also provides your child the chance to meet some of his/her new classmates.

- Some teachers provide basic information at this gathering about their class, as well as sign-up sheets for volunteer opportunities (this is especially true for younger grades), classroom behavioral expectations, broad outlines of academic goals for the year, and a typical weekly schedule.

- **Meet the teacher—child's job:** Encourage your child to introduce themselves to his/her teacher and explore the classroom. It's important for your child to feel comfortable in his/her home away from home, a space to learn, thrive and grow.

- **Meet the teacher—parents' job:** Introduce yourself to other parents. They are a valuable asset. Research repeatedly shows that successful schools have involved parents. Involved parents talk to one another, learn from one another and work together to improve schools. The best way to make that happen is to meet other parents—lots of them. No one will facilitate this. You have to make it happen by stepping up and doing it yourself. For parents of younger children, hosting an informal gathering at your home is another great way to meet parents. Don't over-think it—just send out an email and invite parents over to chat about the new school year. You'll be amazed how many people show up. Or volunteer to start a class-wide email list. All you need is a sheet of paper and a pen—walk around and ask people to sign it. Again, you'll be amazed how many friends you'll make, and how grateful parents will be to have the chance to connect to other parents.

- **Meet the Teacher—what NOT to do:** It is vitally important NOT to come to this event with a list of grievances, requests or anything resembling a TO DO list for the teacher. Your number one aim at this event is to start building a positive relationship with your teacher and other parents. Ask them what they did this summer.

Make polite conversation. If the teacher is new to the school, offer to help them with anything they might need. Consider this setting your chance to build important and lasting bonds with your child's teacher.

■ **Back To School Night**—Schools typically offer a "Curriculum Night" or "Back to School Night" for parents to meet their child's teacher in the classroom. Students are discouraged from attending these (especially in the younger grades).

■ **Back-to-school night has evolved over time**—it's now often a tightly orchestrated event filled with valuable information. If you have more than one child in the school, you may need to split your time among presentations. Teachers often provide Powerpoint or active board presentations to walk the parents through the entire year of academic programming, including major projects, field trips, and homework expectations. Teachers also explain their classroom behavior expectations, particularly for younger grades.

■ **What to look for?** By the end of the back-to-school night, as a parent you should have a reasonably good indication of the teaching and education philosophy of your child's teacher. This isn't as complex as it sounds—mostly, what you are trying to gauge as a parent is what makes your child's teacher tick. Maybe they'll describe a book that captures their outlook on education. Or, sometimes teachers will explain why they became a teacher. Mostly, as a parent, look for clues as to what the teacher is like, and get a sense of his/her strengths. This person will be an integral part of your child's life. Understanding what they are like, what motives them, how they like to communicate and how to engage them will put you and your child on a path to a successful year.

■ Also, at back-to-school night, take a look around the classroom. Is there an organization system in place that can be managed by your child? What does the classroom look like? Will your child be able to navigate it independently each morning and at dismissal? There should be a system for turning in completed homework and assignments each day, taking home items needed for homework, and writing down homework and long-term project assignments. Many teachers do this in a web-based format—with a class website. But no matter what system a teacher uses, time spent setting up an organized classroom and then teaching students how to use it is a small investment with huge payoff. If classrooms save minutes each day because the system for handing out and retrieving information is efficient, that translates into hours of instructional time added on each week, and even days of instruction over the course of the school year. Moreover, an organized classroom will make your life as a parent less stressful—once you master a teacher's operating system, you'll develop a successful routine at home in terms of homework and classwork expectations.

■ **Teacher/Student Questionnaire**—some teachers ask parents to fill out a simple questionnaire at the start of the school year or at P/T conference so that they can get to know your child better. This is a great way for parents to introduce their child to the teacher on a more personal level. It also reflects that the teacher understands the importance of connecting with your child. Here are some sample questions teachers might ask:
  • My child's attitude toward school is ___

- My child expresses the most interest in school when ___
- My child's greatest concern in school seems to be ___
- Some things my child does well are ___
- An area I would like to see my child work especially hard in is ___
- Several subjects/interests/hobbies my child likes are ___

- **Parent/Teacher (P/T) Conferences**—Schools hold one-to-one conferences at regular intervals during the school year (generally two, sometimes three times, per academic year—it's decided through the collective bargaining process). At P/T conferences, the teacher gives the parent and student feedback on the student's performance up to that point in the school year. Parents/students can and should ask any questions or raise any concerns. School districts and principals also allow (and should encourage) parents to request a meeting with their child's teacher at any time if they have an important issue to resolve about their child, typically before or after school on a school day.

- **Student Work Files**—At P/T conference, your child's teacher should have a file of work samples to share with you that reflect both the highlights of work up to that point in the school year, typical work, as well as any concerns. Teachers often share skill inventories, quizzes or other informal assessments they've done to measure student progress (some are district mandated, others are ones that particular teacher likes to use). Writing samples are also important—in elementary school you should always ask for writing samples. If your teacher doesn't provide work samples at P/T conference, ask for them. If they don't have them ready at the time, follow up. This is critical. *If you want to know how your child is doing, you must monitor* *more than just report card grades.* In fact, daily work, quizzes and informal assessments provide a much more well-rounded view of how a child is doing in school than a single grade on a report card or a state test score (although those are important too, but for different reasons).

- **Student Goals**—some districts require students to develop their own personalized goals or student learning plans that focus on different areas of growth. The aim is to make the parent/teacher conference more student-oriented, and more forward looking. If your district does this, that's a great sign. If it doesn't, consider asking them. Student goals provide a way to individualize the education process.

- **Other Skills and Attributes**—there is more to raising a winning student than good grades or high test scores. Certain skills are vital to long-term success, but aren't taught in isolation and aren't necessarily purely academic in focus. These include interdisciplinary skills and attributes like problem solving and working well with others. Some school districts grade students in these areas formally on a report card; others provide more informal feedback. Regardless of what your district does, as a parent you should encourage development of these skills at home, and talk about how your child is doing in these areas with his/her teacher. Also, a working knowledge of why these skills are vital for success will impress your child's teacher, and show him/her that understand the big picture when it comes to education.

- **How to prepare for P/T Conference**—parents should prepare a list of questions and concerns and bring it with him to P/T conference. Some school districts offer guidelines for parents. This a sample of useful questions for parents to consider asking (depending on your child's age and situation), from the Lake Washington School District website:

- At what level is my child working in major subjects?
- What are the reasons he/she is at a particular level?
- What work do you expect my child to cover during the year?
- Does my child arrive in the classroom on time, calm and ready for work?
- Does he/she contribute worthwhile information to the class?
- Does my child attempt to seek more than his/her share of the teacher and class's attention?
- Does my child work and play well with other members of the class and with other children on the playground?
- Is my child developing good work and study habits?
- Is he/she emotionally mature? What can I do to help with social and emotional growth during the year?
- How can I help you? (parents must always ask this question)

So, you've gone to all the mandated conferences, put your best foot forward, met other parents, and it's only October. How does all that translate into ensuring your child receives attention in class?

By taking these steps, you've laid the foundation for a productive relationship with your child's teacher. That's the best way to ensure your teacher knows your child. Instead of your child being one of many faces in the classroom, your child will come to class in way that connects him/her to the teacher because you, as his parent, have fostered the relationship. Building that strong relationship makes everyone involved with your child a stakeholder, and that's how students succeed. Your child's teacher will know that there is a support structure at home reinforcing the learning process at school. This means that when issues arise during the school year (and they will) the teacher won't wrongly assume there's no support at home. Instead the teacher will know they have a partner in learning with you. And, when things are going well, that same teacher will know they have the green light to forge ahead.

HOW TO MAKE THE TEACHER YOUR ALLY

Your teacher is an important ally. We treat allies as partners. That means everyone involved has a shared aim and mutual respect. In this instance, the shared aim is educating your children and helping them reach their potential.

It's important to develop a regular feedback loop with your child's teacher. Parents must keep in mind that teachers are busy juggling the needs of twenty-five or more students, their administrators, and a host of other demands (including parenting, if your teacher has children).

The best way to make an ally of your child's teacher is through regular communication, feedback, and offers of assistance.

1. **Communication:** Parents must remember that communication is a two-way street. *This means parents must read everything that teachers send home and respond to all of it. Every time. No exceptions.* Parents should develop a routine at home of "emptying" the school day's contents (whether it's email or backpack) and responding to it, every school day.

2. **Feedback:** Responses come in two forms.

    i. There are **responses to questions, needs and concerns** (e.g., more pencils, where's the homework, sign the permission slip).

    ii. And there is **feedback from you, the parent,** to let the teacher know what is working. This can be as simple as "My son really likes the novel you all are reading in class" or "I've noticed he's now incorporating more historical references in his writing because of the unit on nonfiction writing you all just completed." Brief email communications such as these let the teacher know that he/she is connecting with your child and with you. It sets up a vital *communications loop* and establishes both trust and camaraderie. It also lets the teacher know that his/her approach is working. **And remember to always keep it brief**—any communication requiring more than a few sentences is better suited for a phone call or in-person conference.

3. **Offers of assistance** typically are appreciated by the teacher. These opportunities present themselves throughout the school year. Even if you can't volunteer during the school day because of work or other commitments, you could help at home with tasks, such as grading quizzes, setting up an email distribution list for the teacher, prep work for class art projects, etc.

4. **Becoming a squeaky wheel:** Most parents understandably dread the prospect of becoming a squeaky wheel at their child's school. The school culture places a premium on cooperation and collaboration. Confrontation is mostly discouraged; this is true even among staff members at a school. Faced with a culture such as this, parents often

find themselves really struggling when their child isn't succeeding at school. They aren't sure where to turn for guidance, or how to even raise the issue.

a. **Up the Ladder**—schools thrive on hierarchies of support, and that hierarchy starts at the local level—the classroom. If you have an issue that isn't resolving itself, you must start by asking for a conference.

b. **Conference**—At this conference, spell out what the issue is. It's important to focus on specific facts and back them up with examples. Here are two examples of how to communicate a common problem in school—note how both are communicating the same problem, but each uses a different approach:

1. "My son won't do his homework. You are assigning too much. Each night we argue about whether to do it, how much he has to do, and who gets to check it. Some evenings we end up in tears. Can you assign less homework for him? Thanks."

2. "I need your help making sure my son is meeting your homework expectations. Right now, we are spending about 60 to 90 minutes each night on assigned math homework (for the past two weeks). To complete homework I must sit right with my son to make sure he stays on task (which means I can't help my other children do their homework). He is really struggling, and it is time consuming. Could we meet to talk about homework expectations as well as the level of independence you'd like to see? Also, can we talk about what your goals are for the homework– finishing work that wasn't done at school? Practicing skills? Learning new material? All of the above? I look forward to speaking with you. Thanks."

a. **Collaborating**—In the first example, the parent makes some good points but doesn't back them up with tangible facts, and frankly comes across as a bit whiny. Also, embedded in that email is an assumption that might later prove false, namely that the teacher is assigning too much homework. Your job as a parent is to marshal relevant facts around the question of homework. To answer that question, you need to consider how much time it takes and whether it can be done with a reasonable amount of help. In the second example, the parent shows that he/she knows their stuff—the message contains lots of useful information about how much time is being spent on homework, how much help is needed and then asks great questions that show the parent wants to understand the "why" behind the homework. The parent demonstrates that he/she isn't going into the exchange with a predetermined conclusion ("too much homework") or specific demand ("assign less") but wants to engage in collaborative problem-solving by identifying a specific issue (spending a lot of time on homework and feeling frustrated) while remaining open to the teacher's thoughts. That's how you build a working partnership. Remember, teachers love collaboration. Use that core competency to work within system while advocating for your child.

b. **Following Up**—After the conclusion of your meeting with the teacher, make sure there is some sort of remedy—a game plan. Always remember to ask for a game plan. While it's great to share ideas, they don't mean much unless they are acted on. The game plan needs to be specific. For the example above, it could be as simple as the teacher assigning only odd- or even-numbered problems on math worksheets. Or giving the child a choice to do the homework at home or during recess at school. But you need a remedy. After the meeting, send a brief "thank you" email to the teacher and confirm the game plan.

c. **But what if the conference doesn't solve anything?** In some instances the conference doesn't solve the problem or even result in modest progress toward solving it. How do you know if that's the case? One rule of thumb is the two-week rule. If, after two weeks, nothing has changed, you should consider following up. How do you know if nothing has changed? Think back to what life was like before the conference. Is life for your student now much different? Have any of the proposed remedies been tried? Has any progress been made? Not necessarily 100 percent success, just some meaningful progress. If not, then it might be time to take it up.

d. **Go to your principal** and ask for a conference. Walk the principal through the problem. Stay focused on facts, like in the example above. It's fine to share your feelings, but do so in a professional way that makes you empathetic. "We're trying to finish homework, but it takes up to 90 minutes each night, and most nights end in tears. It's not working. We're frustrated." The principal can offer other remedies that the teacher can't. These include:

   i.   Observing the teacher in class and providing feedback.

   ii. Bringing in district-level or school-based resources, such as additional instructional help or training, that the teacher might not be inclined to seek out.

   iii. Suggest alternative strategies to the teacher that he/she might not have considered. This is where the experience of the principal can make a huge difference.

e. **Central office**—Some issues are so significant that they can't be resolved at the building level. In these cases, it might be necessary for the parent to seek resolution at the district level. While each district is organized using different nomenclature, districts typically are divided into sections or "communities." Your school will be assigned to a particular division/community, and a district coordinator will be responsible for overseeing all the schools in that community.

f. **How do you know** whether an issue warrants a visit to the district? There is no ready-made formula to answer this question. As a parent you'll build up a reservoir of judgment to help you discern which issues are impor-tant enough to take all the way up to the district level. It should be reserved only for truly significant issues— ones that will change important outcomes for your child. It should never be used to settle a personal score or prove a point. Parents who constantly take issues before their district risk losing credibility quickly. And as a parent, your credibility is the most important cur-rency you have to spend—it's finite, and can be used up quickly for the wrong reasons if parents aren't judicious. It's all about picking the right battles, learning what to ignore, and trying to make the best of the situation.

5. **Homework**—Homework is an issue that generates a lot of passion. Before jumping into the homework wars, parents should do some homework of their own.

a. **District or school policies**—Many districts have man-dated policies or guidelines about homework. Schools typically publish guidelines and recommendations for homework for parents based on district-mandated guidelines. Here is a sample from one elementary school:

Kindergarten: Explore their world and be read to daily.
Grade 1: 15 min, 4 times per week/60 minutes weekly
Grade 2: 20 min, 4 times per week/80 minutes weekly
Grade 3: 30 min, 4 times per week/120 minutes weekly
Grade 4: 40 min, 4 times per week/160 minutes weekly
Grade 5: 50 min, 4 times per week/200 minutes weekly
Grade 6: 60 min, 4 times per week/240 minutes weekly

b. **Homework policies**—Many teachers comply with homework policies by assigning nightly independent reading of the child's choice. Other teachers prefer homework packets due at the end of the week. Still others assign homework on a daily basis to address various needs. Schools try to be flexible with parents. If your child needs a regular exception to homework parents should address this early in a parent/teacher conference.

c. **Homework rationale**—It's important for parents to figure out what the teacher's homework philosophy is. Here are some common rationales:

    i. **Skill practice**—This might consist of math worksheets or handwriting practice.

    ii. **Covering new material**—Some teachers assign chapters of a textbook to read at home to introduce new material for students prior to in-class discussion (e.g., "Read chapter 22 of the social studies textbook and be prepared to discuss").

    iii. **Independent project work**—As students get older, they are expected to work on independent projects. Some homework might involve gathering resource materials, interviewing experts, and otherwise gathering information needed to complete the project. Teachers typically try to balance allowing time in class to work on the project with some expectation of work outside of class.

iv. **Completion of in-class work**—If a student doesn't complete assigned work in class, the teacher might ask that the student finish it at home.

d. **Online homework and class assignment monitoring**—Some districts now use online tools to help parents and students keep track of in-class work, homework, tests, quizzes, and projects. Teachers enter grades for all assigned work online in your child's account—parents and the student have access to that account (but not those of their classmates). If an assignment isn't turned in, the teacher scores it as "incomplete," provides a brief explanation (e.g., "student didn't turn in during class; student asked for extension," etc.). This type of tool is an invaluable asset for parents and teachers. It eliminates the need for multiple email inquiries to the teacher. It prevents students from giving inconsistent versions of events to the parent and teacher trying to explain why homework or class work wasn't completed. It's all recorded online for the teacher, parent, and student to see. It also eliminates every parent's worst nightmare scenario of discovering at report card time that his/her child hasn't been turning in assignments the entire grading period. At the high school level, parents can also keep track online of their student's progress toward completing graduation credit requirements. Various companies provide this type of service. In the state of Washington, a commonly used one is Skyward, Inc.

e. **The homework wars**—There are numerous research studies and articles questioning the efficacy of heavy homework loads, particularly for younger grades. Critics have questioned the value of "busy work" homework, while proponents stress the development of good work habits as laying a necessary foundation for high school work. Rather than choose sides in this battle, parents should instead focus on what type of homework meets the needs of their child. Some students require more skill practice. Others need to work independently on projects over time to learn time management skills. The best approach is to talk to your teacher, while being mindful of your child's learning style. Many teachers are flexible and will listen to your concerns. Figure out what the teacher wants to accomplish with homework. That will help you as a parent develop appropriate strategies at home.

12

HOW THE SCHOOL SYSTEM WORKS

To a parent the school bureaucracy can be a daunting monolith. When you have a problem or a question, just figuring out where to start can be a challenge. In this piece, attorney and parent advocate, **BETH SIGALL** gives you the 411 on how most districts are organized. Remember, the first place to start is with your child's teacher and/or principal. But if you don't find satisfaction or your question is a larger districtwide one, then you have to find your way through the maze of the district office organization. If you are fortunate, your school district may have a parent advocate or ombudsman. Ask if there's someone who works with parents on questions and issues first. If there isn't a dedicated person, then follow the ideas laid out in Beth's piece. But never give up!

—Marc Sachnoff, Chief Parent, The Parents Union

HOW THE SCHOOL SYSTEM WORKS

BY BETH SIGALL

Who is in charge? To understand how your school system works you must understand its structure. There are two major players in a school system—the school board and school district administration (a third major player is the teachers' union).

School Board—School board members are (typically) elected for set terms by voters residing in the school district. They function as the "governors" of the school district. Board members (sometimes called directors) provide implementation and oversight of district policies and procedures, in accordance with state and federal law. They adopt new policies and make recommendations in response to the evolving needs of students and the greater education community. The Lake Washington School District offers a good overview of the main areas of focus for a school board.

They are:

1. **Vision**—focuses the work on student achievement through a comprehensive strategic planning process
2. **Structure**—provides prudent financial planning and oversight; diligent and innovative policymaking
3. **Accountability**—sets specific goals and a process for evaluation, reporting and recommendations for improvements
4. **Advocacy**—champions public education in the local community and before state and federal policy makers

Here is a sample School Board Governance and Job Description from the Lake Washington School District.

School District Administration—A professional staff of school administrators and employees, led by a superintendent, run the day-to-day functions of the school district. The superintendent is hired by the school board and reports directly to the school board. You might hear this referred to as the "central office" or "the district."

Who makes the rules? Successful school districts establish and follow clear lines of authority and responsibility as to the functions of the elected school board and the professional (not elected) administration. School boards must resist the temptation to micro-manage the daily functioning of the school district or to champion a single issue to satisfy a particular political constituency. They must focus instead on governance and policy for the entire district. School district administrators, and especially the superintendent, must be mindful of their job description as well, which is to provide direction and leadership to the school district administrators and employees on the daily management of the district's programs and services.

The superintendent also provides regular feedback and guidance to the school board. Arguably the most important job of the school board is to choose the right superintendent.

In terms of district operations, the school board works together with the school district administrators in these main areas:

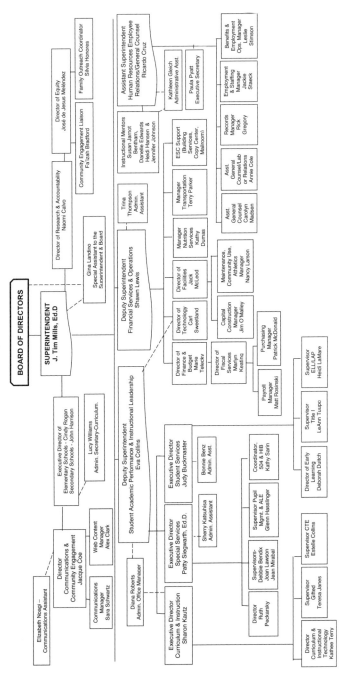

- bond and levy elections
- budget adoption
- facilities
- curriculum adoption
- fiscal planning and oversight
- employee relations
- transportation

b. What are the rules? School district rules are (or should be) published in an accessible fashion on your school district website. District rules touch on the day-to-day operations of the school district at every level. These might include student conduct and school discipline, use of facilities, contract negotiation, personnel, instruction, and other areas.

c. To whom do I talk when I have a problem? Where to turn when you have a problem can be complex, especially for first-timers. Like other large, complex entities, school districts have a multitude of layers, encompassing managers, supervisors and directors of various departments. To further complicate matters, school districts tend to be jargon heavy, which means even if you know what your issue is, it might not be readily apparent which division addresses your need if you don't know the right jargon. Here is an organization chart for the Bellevue School District. www.bsd405.org/portals/0/administration/Superintendent/BSD-org-chart.pdf

As a parent, you may spend a considerable amount of time and effort trying to locate the right person to ask. When you do start asking, never accept "no, that's not my department" as an answer. Be sure to ask "if you can't answer this question, please tell me who can."

The school board as a remedy for students or parents is typically reserved for two main areas:

1. Student conduct—appeals or hearings involving suspension or expulsion for serious infractions of school rules (e.g., violence, drugs, guns, bullying).
2. Changes to district policy impacting your child and similarly situated children (e.g., moving the start times for high school, changes in transportation schedules)

1. **Successful advocacy for your child** at the school board level requires an extraordinary amount of persistence. Working one's way through the bureaucracy of education remains a daunting task. You will repeat the facts surrounding your student's issue to the point of memorization. But School Board and district officials time and again stress that persistence does eventually pay off, as does a pleasant disposition.

2. **Successful advocacy beyond your child**—in some instances you may find that the issue involved is systemic in nature and requires a district-wide policy shift. In those cases, parents can canvass and organize with other parents who are similarly situated. After that, parents can approach school board members individually to discuss the issue. If that approach doesn't resolve the issue, parents can present their needs openly at monthly public school board meetings.

THE PROMISE

Once you understand what your own education story has been and how it impacts your expectations for your children's education, and you have developed some understanding of how your child learns, you can now begin the steps to becoming a true partner in your child's education.

So how do you become a true partner in your child's education? The Parents Union's answer is to start by helping parents and concerned family members become partners with their teacher. And together with the teacher to become partners with our children for their own success.

We've created a simple one page tool that you can use to create this three-way partnership with your child and their teacher. We call it the "Washington Student Success Promise."

"THE PROMISE"

- Creates a triad of trust for your child's school success.
- Establishes transparency and accountability for all three partners.
- Sets clear goals for your child to achieve.
- Opens the door for good communication between parents and teachers.

HOW TO USE THE PROMISE

The more you are willing to become involved in your child's education the more likely they are to succeed in school and in life. This entire book and our entire organization are premised on this belief.

Before you print out and take your copy of The Promise to school for your child's teacher to sign, we suggest you read it over carefully and decide whether or not the points listed for parents are right for you. This is a real accountability tool and if you want to build trust with your kid's teacher(s) you need to make sure you are going to make good on your commitments.

We also suggest that you discuss the points of The Promise with your child. After all, we are asking them to make a commitment too, something they may never have been asked to do so overtly.

Some kids are open and even excited about mom or dad getting involved with their teacher. But others may have a strong interest in keeping us out of the classroom. While this is more prevalent with Middle School and High School kids where blooming independence is expressed in a lack of desire for any kind of parental involvement or interference, we shouldn't hesitate to let our kids know that we are making a change. Talk openly about your desire to be present, to be involved. Listen to what they have to say, their concerns, their hopes and their fears. Remind them that we are there to help them succeed. Use the blanks to fill in ideas for supporting each other towards their success.

Once you and your child are ready to make the commitments and have signed your parts, you are ready to engage your teacher. Give them a call or send an email to set up a time to talk in person. We don't recommend giving The Promise to your child to bring to the teacher – you want to show your face, demonstrate your determination.

When you meet with the teacher, show them The Promise. Let them look it over and then request that they join you in making The Promise to each other for this child's success. Be polite and respectful. This may be the first time they've ever seen The Promise and they may request some time to look it over. if they aren't ready to make their commitment in your first meeting, suggest that you meet again on a specific date and time or that they call you at a specific time to discuss it.

Remember, we are not trying to force teachers into this! We want them to become partners with us in our kid's success in their class. We want to work constructively and build good will.

I f you don't already have one in mind, ask the teacher to suggest a specific academic target for your child and a date by which to accomplish it. Discuss it together with your child and get everyone's agreement.

If you can't get agreement on a specific target, leave it blank for now. Our goal is to get you involved and to build trust. And sometimes building trust takes time.

FOLLOW UP

The Promise is not a onetime document to be signed and ignored. Once everyone has signed it consider putting it on your refrigerator door or other prominent place where you and your child can see it every day.

And let us know that you've started the process with your teacher and student by noting this in your member page on www.theparentsunion.org. or emailing us at ThePromise@TheParentsUnion.org. Why should you do this? First, because we want to know how many parents are using The Promise and second: we want to identify and recognize those teachers who are working in partnership with parents in our Educator Honor Roll.

Check in with your teacher frequently – at least once a month by phone or email. Find out how your child is doing and how you can support their improvement. And of course attend your parent - teacher conference and consider having your child attend as well. That's your opportunity to check in with the teacher on the commitments of The Promise. Its also a time to see where you are in relation to the specific academic goal you've set with the teacher and if your child is on track to accomplish it by the target date. And if they aren't on target, talk to the teacher about what each of you can do to make it happen.

And at the end of the year do two things:

1. Thank the teacher for working with you in partnership for your child's success. And together recognize the progress your child has made – even if you didn't accomplish the goal, celebrate any real progress made.
2. Email us at ThePromise@theparentsunion.org and let us know your experience with The Promise. What worked, what didn't' and what do you think we should change in future versions?

What if the Teacher Just Won't Participate in The Promise with Me?

Almost all teachers want to work with parents in partnership towards student improvement. But if you encounter a teacher who simply does not want you in the classroom, or doesn't want to work together with you on The Promise, then you have a couple of choices…

1. You can ask the teacher if they are willing to propose some kind of alternative compact that specifies each or your roles with accountability for all parties.
2. You can discuss your concerns with the Principal or other school leader.
3. And if your teacher is really resistant to parent partnerships, you can organize other parents and begin the road to change through advocacy.

WASHINGTON STUDENT SUCCESS PROMISE

Elementary School Version

Message to Teachers

As a teacher you play an essential role with parents in helping students reach their highest potential. We believe that creating positive and active relationships between parents, teachers, and students is essential to that goal. The Washington Student Success Promise is a tool to help you help this student succeed. Join hundreds of teachers across the state this year in making The Promise for a brighter future not just for each student, but for all students in Washington State.

Message to Parents and Families

Parents are powerful! Your involvement in your child's education is a crucial factor in their success in school and in life. You are your child's first teacher and you lead by example every day through your attitudes and actions about school and learning. That's why it is important to regularly engage your child in conversation about what they are learning in school. The Promise is a tool to help you help your student succeed. By creating a positive partnership with your child's teacher and by following the points of The Promise, you can open the way for your child to improve their grades, their attendance, and even their behavior.

Message to students

You have a mission -- a mission to become the best you can be. By uniting together with your parents or guardian and with your teacher you can get the most out of school. By really challenging yourself you can continue to grow and discover strengths and talents that you never even knew existed in you. If you fall down, get up again and keep trying. And when you need help (and we all need help sometimes) the people who signed this Promise have committed themselves to supporting you and helping you win.

The Parents Union

The Student Success Promise is brought to you by The Parents Union. Our mission is to inform, empower and unite parents into a broad base of power towards the goal of a world class education for every child in Washington State. Join Now - www.TheParentsUnion.org

THE WASHINGTON STUDENT PROMISE

We all want a world class education for our children. Despite the many challenges facing education in our state, the only thing we know that really works is a great teacher, engaged parent(s), a motivated student – and open communication between all three. To that end I am requesting that you join me in making "The Promise" to me, to my child, and to our community.

I [name of parent], parent of [name of student] at [name of school]:

❑ Promise I will take personal responsibility for my child's success in school.

❑ Promise I will ensure my child knows what his school work is, understands how to accomplish it, and when it is due.

❑ Promise I will treat my child's teacher with respect and participate in parent/teacher conferences and classroom activities and respond to teacher emails/calls within 48 hours.

❑ Promise I will ensure my child arrives at school on time every day, ready to learn.

❑ Promise I will create a culture of love for learning in our home by reading to and with my child.

❑ _____ [fill in your own promise point]

I [name of teacher], [x grade] teacher of [name of student]:

❑ Promise I will always treat this student with compassion and respect.

❑ Promise I will provide him/her with individual attention required to meet their academic goals and reach their highest potential.

❑ Promise I will work in partnership with this student's parents in a welcoming and respectful way.

❑ Promise I will give meaningful feedback to this student and parent when the student does well and when they need additional support.

❑ Promise I will respond to parent emails/calls within 48 hours.

❑ _____ [fill in your own promise point]

I [student]:

❑ Promise I will do my best on each assignment.

❑ Promise that if I need help, I will ask my parents and/or my teacher for help

❑ Promise I will come to school every morning ready to learn.

❑ Promise I will treat my teacher, my parents and my classmates with respect.

❑ _____ [fill in your own promise point]

Shared academic goal(s) for this student:

To accomplish _____ by _____ [time frame]

_____   _____   _____
Parent/Guardian   Teacher   Student
Date: _____   Date: _____   Date: _____

Note: Once The Promise is signed by everyone, post this on your refrigerator or home bulletin board where you and your child can see it every day.

When I first took our daughter to the school office to talk about her absence from first grade, I met the most influential person in the building. Not the principal, not the counselor, not the librarian or any teacher—it was the school office secretary. And she was not a friendly person. While I was trying to figure out what form I needed to fill out with little help her, another school employee came in and said hello to me. This recognition perked my daughter up. I looked at the secretary and remarked offhand-edly that I'd helped paint the lockers and fences over the summer. Her face changed and the form appeared almost immediately. Moral: as one of our favorite teachers, **CHRIS EIDE** shares in this piece, you need to know "who's who in the zoo."

—Marc Sachnoff, Chief Parent, The Parents Union

HOW SCHOOLS WORK

BY CHRIS EIDE

Although nearly every one of us has experience with school as a student, interacting with schools as an adult is different. As a parent, you are there to advocate for your child and his or her education. It is important to remember that although schools tend to be a part of a larger system, you are still going to be working with real people at the school level. Here are some things you should know before you call or go to the school:

1) Learn about the school's modes of communication.
   a. Sometimes schools will send home newsletters or other forms of communication with students. It is best to know when to expect these communications so that you can remind your child to deliver them.

b. Schools often establish email lists in order to communicate with parents. If you have access to email, ask to be added to any email lists.

c. Visit your school's website often to look for what's happening.

2) If your child is having a problem in elementary school, it is best to first contact their teacher. If they are having a problem in middle or high school, it is best to first contact either their teacher or the school's counselor.

a. In elementary school, your child's teacher is the best point person because he is with all of the students for most of the day and is likely very aware of the dynamics between students. They are typically used to helping solve problems between students as well.

b. In middle and high school, teachers are only with each student for a portion of the day, so their knowledge of interpersonal dynamics will be less than an elementary school teacher's. Middle and high schools typically have counselors who are versed in conflict resolution. If there is an incident that happens outside of class, counselors will be more informed and are tasked with handling confidential information.

3) The secretary is an important friend to have.

a. As in life, relationships are very important. The school's secretary is often the keeper of the schedules for the administrators (principal, assistant principal, dean), which means that if you want to see the principal, you will likely have to go through the secretary.

4) Some rules come from the district, while other rules are often made at each school.

a. Be sure and learn about the expectations of the school and how they might be different from other schools. School leaders will often try to set their school apart by pushing more rigorous academic or behavioral standards.

b. Visit the district's website to learn about district behavior guidelines for students to make sure that you know that your child is being treated fairly at their school.

5) The principal makes most final decisions regarding the school and students.

a. The principal is the head of the school. He or she is in charge of making decisions about teachers and other administrators. When teachers, counselors, or other administrators can't solve issues involving students, the principal will in most cases make the final decision. If it is an issue that is bigger than what the school is capable of dealing with, officials in the central office may make the final decision.

Most important, you should always remember that adults working at schools want what is best for your child just as you do, and the best path is to work together to solve any problems that may arise. Build positive relationships with teachers, administrators, counselors, and especially the secretary. If it seems that they are making decisions that aren't putting your child first, remember that they are also considering how to best serve the whole class of students. Stay positive, and work together with school personnel and your child to find the best solution.

13

WHAT YOU CAN DO IF YOU BELIEVE THE SCHOOL IS UNSAFE

Bullying is one of the topics of highest concern with parents I talk to these days. Identifying it, understanding it and preventing it are challenges to all of us as parents. And even more so when it's our child that accused of being a bully. While there doesn't yet seem to be a magic bullet to solve it, **JOE NEWMAN**, a cutting edge behaviorist and intervention specialist, brings new ideas to the subject that are worth thinking about.

—Marc Sachnoff, Chief Parent, The Parents Union

RAISING LIONS

(adapted from *Raising Lions*, by Joe Newman)

Bullying at School

On January 14, 2010, fifteen-year-old Phoebe Prince committed suicide after suffering months of constant bullying from school classmates. This was only the latest of a string of extreme bullying incidents becoming more prevalent in public schools.

The continued increase in the frequency and intensity of bullying is a result of several things. First, there has been a cultural shift in today's children toward much stronger feelings of omnipotence (a strong self-recognition and a weak recognition of others) than in children of the past. One of the consequences of this is that children feel a stronger pull toward satisfying their own needs and feelings than respecting the needs and feelings of others. Combine this with the lower capacity for intimacy (due to the lack of healthy mutual recognition) and a child's already strong desire for social status and power, and the result is more children who are willing to be cruel in order to impress and belong to a group.

The third problem is our assumption that bullies act in ways that are inappropriate and cruel because they lack an intellectual understanding about right and wrong. So we respond with conversation (when school bullying gets out of hand therapists are sent in to talk with children about the effects of bullying and why it is wrong). Bullies don't lack a cognitive understanding of why their actions are wrong. The truth is they are acting this way because on some level it gets them the social power they crave. If we respond to bullying with swift, strong consequences that reduce their social power, instead of more talk, then bullying will stop. Moralizing to them only makes the gap between you and them wider and feeds the "cool factor" of their social power with their friends.

In order to stop bullying it is necessary to respond with action consequences that remove the incentive as soon as the first signs of bullying appear. When this is done swiftly and consistently, then a culture of bullying won't have a chance to take root and grow, never mind grow to the levels of cruelty we've recently seen at our schools.

The short version: respond to bullying immediately with more action and less talk.

RESOURCES

- Empowering Parents website:
  http://www.empoweringparents.com/My-Child-is-Being-Bullied.php#

- Kidshealth website: http://kidshealth.org/parent/emotions/behavior/bullies.html

Discovering that your child is being bullied has got to be one of our worst nightmares. The feelings of helplessness. Knowing your child is being tormented. Wanting to solve it for them, protect them, confront the bully. All these feelings can run through our heads when bullying rears its ugly head. In this piece, we present an interview conducted by **ELISABETH WILKINS**, editor of the online-content site, Empowering Parents, with Peggy Moss, a nationally known expert on bullying and a tireless advocate for the prevention of hate violence. She is also the author of *Say Something*, an award-winning children's book that helps parents and educators start conversations with kids about actions they can take when they are being bullied or witness other kids being tormented at school. Peggy brings a straight forward "how to" approach that you can start using right now to determine if your child is being bullied and what to do about it.

—Marc Sachnoff, Chief Parent, The Parents Union

MY CHILD IS BEING BULLIED—WHAT SHOULD I DO?

BY ELISABETH WILKINS, EMPOWERING PARENTS EDITOR

(reprinted with permission from www.empoweringparents.com — www.empoweringparents.com/My-Child-is-Being-Bullied.php?&key=Bullying)

Are name-calling and teasing just part of growing up, a rite of passage that all kids go through? "Many people out there think that adults are making too much of a fuss about it, that we should leave kids to their own devices. We know better now," argues Peggy. "I have talked to 80-year-olds who remember the name of the person who tormented them in school, and the name of the child who stood up for them in first grade. This is pain that has lasted a lifetime. We have the information to stop bullying now, so why wouldn't we?"

HOW CAN YOU TELL IF YOUR CHILD IS BEING BULLIED?

There's a good chance your kid won't walk up to you and say, "I'm getting teased and bullied at school, the kids are calling me names." Instead, it's going to manifest itself by your child saying, "I don't want to go to school today." If this seems to be happening a lot, consider the possibility that bullying might be the reason behind the sick days. Also, look for signs that kids are hurting themselves. Self-mutilation can be a sign. For boys, one classic symptom is that they are teased so much about being gay or being atypical that they're terrified to go to the bathroom. Since there's only one way in and one way out of a bathroom, it's an ideal place to tease other kids. Boys who are bullied often won't go all day, which can lead to lifelong intestinal issues. This could potentially be a sign—if your kid races home and goes to the bathroom every day after school. These are all possible signals that your child might be the target of teasing at school.

As a parent, teacher or health care worker, add "Bullying" to your radar when you're trying to figure out what's going on with a child—add the possibility that your kid is getting tormented at school. The injury is real when kids get teased—unchecked, it can be devastating.

IF MY CHILD COMES TO ME AND TELLS ME HE IS BEING BULLIED, WHAT IS THE BEST THING TO DO?

I would say let your child talk about it. Don't say, "What did you do that made them tease you?" That's a pit parents can fall into.

Don't make the assumption that your kid has done something to bring on the teasing. Teasing isn't always logical, and for your kid it doesn't matter why—it just matters that it's happening.

Listen in a non-judgmental way about your child *and* about the teaser. Let your kid do the talking. Don't try to solve the problem. Ask, "What happened? How did that make you feel?" to draw your child out. And try to find out more about the kid who's doing the teasing. Don't say, "Oh my God, what a rotten kid," because you're just getting a part of the story. Your child doesn't need you to go ballistic or take on the problem as your own. Your child needs to know that he's being heard and that his feelings matter. Once you've got the whole story out, depending upon what's happened, you can take your next step. For a parent to be explosive about the situation will cause a child to recoil. If I march to school and confront the bully on the playground, my child is not going to feel safe telling me anything about this again. I'm taking on his battle for him.

SO, WHAT CAN I DO TO STOP THE BULLYING?

The short answer is to let your kid come up with ideas. Ask him questions like, "What do you think you can say next time? What do you think might work?" Help your child see what the outcome might be of their words and actions; help them see that this is a problem they can solve on their own terms. For example, your kid might come up with the idea of saying to the bully, "Leave me alone, you jerk." Instead of the parent saying, "That's a bad idea," respond with, "What do you think is going to happen if you do that?" Let them figure out that the bullying might escalate if they resort to name-calling.

Your child might then shrug and say, "I could walk away from the bully." You can suggest that they walk away the first time and say what they need to say the next time. We have to be honest about how hard it is to face a tormentor. It's also important to ask your child this question: "What's going to make *you* feel better about this situation?" But make sure you're not the one coming up with the solution. It's important that your child feels like they're solving the problem on his or her own terms. It's a skill you can teach them that will last a lifetime.

WHAT IF MY CHILD *WON'T* TALK TO ME ABOUT BEING BULLIED?

As long as they feel like they have a safe place to go, that is what's important. And if you feel your kid can't talk to you, swallow hard and say, "OK, my child is not talking to me, but *they've got to talk*." Put someone else in that room with them that they can talk to, whether it's an aunt or uncle, teacher, counselor, coach or family friend. Unless that conversation can start, it's very hard to get to the heart of the problem.

WHEN SHOULD I APPROACH MY CHILD'S TEACHERS ABOUT IT?

Go in pretty early, as soon as your child starts coming home and mentioning that they are being teased. If your kid is coming home more than once a week and saying, "These kids are teasing me and I don't like to go to the bathroom," go in after school when all the kids are gone. Call the teacher and set up an appointment. Teachers are like everyone else, if you mention something in passing, it won't carry as much weight. If you make an appointment, they will listen.

A caution to parents: often when your kid is getting bullied, their teachers don't know it. Kids are smart enough not to do it in front of the teacher. Bear in mind that when you go to a teacher you shouldn't be carrying a hatchet in your back pocket. It may not be that the teacher is doing a bad job, it might mean it's happening out of earshot. Don't go into school assuming that you'll be received with, "Oh yes, we've seen this happening." Say things like, "My child is coming home and talking about this." And then say, "This is how it's impacting my child." That's what teachers need to know, because it may not be obvious to them. What you're asking is for them to keep an eye out. Later, you can check in with email, and they can get back to you when you're ready. If the bullying doesn't stop, or it's really bad bullying, you should go to the principal. A really great trick is to go in with a question: "I talked to Ms. Fabbiano a week ago, and my daughter is still coming home with this complaint. What should I do?" Put it into the lap of the principal and ask, "When can I expect to hear back from you about what you've done? What's the next step?" Then you can tell your child that you will be getting an answer on Thursday about what steps will be taken. It's also all right to ask educators to keep your conversations private, and then you can reassure your child about this as well.

WHAT ABOUT WHEN IT'S GONE BEYOND VERBAL ABUSE AND THERE IS A PHYSICAL THREAT?

Once you've got a threat, you've got a crime—it's called "Criminal Threatening." It's time to alert the police. You want to be in touch with the school long before you've got a threat of violence. When the threat of violence comes, you're in police territory. That's why there's so much uproar about teasing and bullying, because once a child has been threatened with violence, it's a really big wound. It's hard to tell that child that they can feel safe at school ever again. Especially if the threat is anonymous. For the kid who gets an anonymous threat, going to school is terrifying minute-to-minute. There is no way a child can focus on her math test if she's trying to figure out who wrote the note saying they were going to kill her. By the time you get to that point, you are in crisis mode.

Part of it is getting a sense from teachers about what's really going on in that school. As a parent, it's much more complicated. If you can't figure out who is making the threat and the police can't figure it out, you really have to decide whether the child is safe in the school and whether you want to keep her there.

The message to kids in your book *Say Something* is that kids have the power to stop bullying behavior at school themselves. Can you explain how this works?

When we talk to kids about bullies, remind them of this truth: Bullies are cowards.

Most bullies won't tease two kids together, and almost never will they pick on three kids at once. Even in a group, bullies single out one or two kids. In terms of plain old teasing, bullies like to put other kids down, to make someone else feel lousy so they can feel powerful. Most kids who are teasing and putting down other kids are looking for approval from peers. Teach your kids that there are a lot of ways to show that you don't approve. If someone just speaks up and says, "Whoa," or "Ew," or "That's not cool," it can be effective. If another kid can walk up and say, "Hey, come over here, you want to go play?" to the person getting picked on, that's huge. It often will defuse the whole situation. That bully is unlikely to follow, and he has just been told in public that what he's doing is not cool. Whether a teacher or kid breaks the assumption, now the kid getting picked on knows that not everyone agrees, and so does the bully. It doesn't always have to take a lot of courage. Kids should know that they have the power to change their situation, especially when they work together.

For more information about Peggy Moss, see www.SaySomethingNow.com.

14

RAISING THE WHOLE CHILD

Parents are always talking about kids and food. And food is often the source of a lot of tension, tears and fighting in our homes. But it doesn't have to be that way. We can bring our kids into the process of choosing what we eat, shopping for it and cooking it. Nutritionist **LORI BRIZEE** has some great practical tips on how to inform and involve kids in our food choices in ways that make the process less stressful and even enjoyable.

—Marc Sachnoff, Chief Parent, The Parents Union

TEACHING KIDS ABOUT HEALTHY EATING

(excerpted from *Healthy Choices, Healthy Children,*

by Lori Brizee)

Our kids learn their eating habits from us, their parents, more than anyone else. Yes, they learn about nutrition in preschool and school, but what they see and learn at home has the most sticking power!

If they see us eating on the run, skipping meals, grabbing chips and soda pop for our snacks, they will see those habits as normal adult eating.

Three incredibly easy steps to healthy eating

Step 1: Model healthy eating for your children

How we, as adults, eat is more important than anything else; nothing we say to our kids will override what they see us do. The same goes for any other health message we want to give to our kids—it is difficult for them to believe that smoking is a problem, for example, if they see us smoking; it is difficult for them to see exercise is important if we are physically inactive.

Step 2: Talk to your kids about why you are making different family food choices

Tell them why you buy dried fruit rather than fruit snacks; why you buy whole grain bread rather than white bread; why you don't buy potato chips and cheese puffs very often; why you insist on a piece of fruit and a vegetable in their school lunches; why you use the really small dishes or teacups for ice cream rather than the cereal bowls; why you don't buy apple juice or juice boxes. Our kids see what others are eating and they want to fit in; it can be helpful for them to understand why their lunches or snacks might look different.

When you are at the grocery store, talk to your kids about why you are buying certain products:

Local and in-season fruits and vegetables versus imported or out-of-season. Foods that are local and seasonal can be picked at a riper stage, do not sit in storage for transportation for as long a time, and thus tend to be higher in nutrients.

Oatmeal in a large box or in bulk versus packets of instant oatmeal. Plain oatmeal is a great high-fiber, very low sugar cereal, but the little instant packets have lots of added salt and sugar. You can add apples, cinnamon, and raisins and a little sugar to plain oatmeal and have a much healthier breakfast than if you eat instant apple raisin cinnamon oatmeal. (This is also a great way to give them an economics lesson—the larger boxes or bulk oatmeal costs much less per serving than the instant stuff does.)

Lean meats, chicken, turkey, and fish versus fatty meats such as ribs, prime steaks, bacon, or sausage. The fatty meats have more saturated fat and cholesterol, which are not good for our hearts. The very lean meats give us plenty of protein and iron and vitamins, with far less fat.

We make lots of decisions at the grocery store based on nutritional value. Talking about it helps reinforce the lessons our kids get by watching us eat a healthy diet.

Step 3: Involve your kids in food decisions
At the grocery store, teach your kids how to pick quality fruits and vegetables and how to choose healthy cereals and packaged foods.

Have your kids help to plan meals at home. If you have decided on a specific main dish for dinner, let kids plan the vegetables and/or fruits—green salad, cooked vegetables, cut raw vegetables, fruit salad, plate of sliced fruit, or a combination of any of the above. Let them decide on other side dishes—roasted yams or potatoes, brown rice, whole grain pasta, quinoa, whole-wheat couscous. Let kids plan their school-day breakfasts and lunches. Require some basic healthy parameters such as: a whole grain, a protein, a fruit and/or vegetable, and milk or water.

Encourage your kids to participate in all levels of food preparation:

- **Gardening**—Many kids truly have no idea where their foods come from. Growing at least a few foods at home gives kids a whole new understanding of what it takes to get food on the table. Don't have a yard? Try container gardening for tomatoes, peppers, green beans, and other suitable vegetables.

- **Grocery shopping**—Allow young children to put produce in bags and take foods off the store shelves and put them in the cart. Give your older kids and teenagers a list and a basket and ask them to find those foods and meet you at a specific location in the store. You will get the grocery shopping done faster and prepare your kids to do it themselves by the time they can drive to the store for you! (Make sure you retain veto power over the items in their carts. You might negotiate with them to choose one treat that is not necessarily "healthy"—just give them a price and size limit.)

- **Storage**—Make sure that you include unloading the car and putting foods away as part of your kids' grocery shopping experience. Teach them to put the newest foods in the back of the refrigerator or cupboards and the older foods in front or on top of the new foods. This will likely require rearranging of the vegetable and fruit drawers of your fridge and shelves in your cupboards, which they might not want to take time to do, but it is part of the process!

- **Food preparation**—Your kids have helped to plan meals, so now let them do as much preparation as they can. Preschoolers can tear the lettuce for green salad and pour ingredients into a bowl or pan. They can also help by setting and clearing the table. Five- to eight-year-olds can get ingredients out of the cupboards and refrigerator, stir things on the stove with very close supervision, make sandwiches, and load and unload the dishwasher. By the time a child is nine years old, he is capable of cooking simple meals (macaroni and cheese from scratch, spaghetti sauce, scrambled eggs) with supervision while using the stove. By middle-school age, a child can prepare a meal without supervision, as long as they have grown up learning how to use the stove and knives safely.

- **Cleanup**—No one has truly learned how to cook unless they have learned to clean up. Even if your kids have worked very hard to prepare a meal, they need to be involved in the cleanup (at least cleaning up their cooking mess). Teaching them some clean-as-you-cook techniques can be very useful in the long run.

My mother's claim to fame was that each of her children could put a meal on the table by themselves at nine years of age (she really didn't like cooking, and teaching us to cook was a way for her to do less of it!). Because of that, I developed a love of cooking. I took that idea to heart and made sure that my kids learned to cook, starting at an early age. By the time they were middle-schoolers, I could leave them with instructions on what to make for dinner and have a great meal prepared by the time I walked in the door from work! Even moms who love cooking need a reprieve once in a while.

At the same time that you are teaching your kids meal planning and preparation, you are also giving them nutrition lessons. They will get some nutrition education at school; that will reinforce what you have already taught.

ACTIONS FOR THE WEEK

Choose one or two that you are not already doing

1. Ask one of your kids to help plan menus and grocery shop for the week. If you have more than one child, alternate who helps with the planning. Besides being educational, it gives you one-on-one time with each child.
2. Take one of your children to the grocery store with you and talk about what you are buying and why.
3. Give each child a job related to meal preparation at least one day this week—setting the table, making one or more parts of a meal, making lunches, clearing the table, and helping with the dishes.
4. Give your older children a list that includes 25 to 50 percent of what you need to buy at the grocery store. Give them a set amount of time to gather the items and then meet you at a designated place in the store.

NUTRITION AND LIFESTYLE REFERENCES FOR FAMILIES

http://centraloregonnutrition.com/meet-lori-brizee/ — To contact author and nutritionist Lori Brizee

http://www.eatright.org/public — This is the public page of the American Dietetic Association's website

http://www.letsmove.gov — First Lady Michelle Obama's website gives practical ideas for healthy eating and physical activity in the lives of our kids

http://www.choosemyplate.gov — A government website that gives detailed information about food and activity needs for individuals of all ages

MAHATMA GANDHI is famously quoted as saying, "We must be the change we wish to see in the world." But what does an Indian nonviolence advocate who died more than sixty years ago have to do with raising winning students in the twenty-first century?

In a word—everything!

Gandhi's approach to nonviolent change contains within it the seeds to creating a happy, harmonious family, solving the crisis of bullying, and even transforming the culture of materialism that our kids (and we as parents) are often caught up in. Today, the most active living link to Gandhi's legacy lives in—of all places—Rochester, New York. Arun Gandhi is Mohandas K. Gandhi's grandson and heads up The M.K. Gandhi Institute for Nonviolence. In this piece excerpted from Arun's book, *Legacy of Love*, he provides us with clear tools to deconstruct violence, and help us and our children neutralize and transform the ever-escalating poisons of conflict, hatred and aggression. No Formula To Nonviolence

An important thing to remember in the practice of nonviolence is that one must not be dogmatic. Because Grandfather used method A to effect change in a certain situation, it does not mean that method A can be used in similar situations. In nonviolence there is no formula, as there is in violent solutions, where one can institutionalize fixed responses. This is, perhaps, a shortcoming of the "three strikes and you're out" rule of American criminal justice. Nonviolence requires one to be innovative, to shape one's response according to each unique set of circumstances. The possibilities are endless.

—Marc Sachnoff, Chief Parent, The Parents Union

LOOKING AT NONVIOLENCE

(Excerpted from *Legacy of Love*, by Arun Gandhi)

AN EYE FOR AN EYE

n western society justice has come to mean revenge, "an eye for an eye." It is so ingrained in us that we do not have a sense of closure unless someone is made to pay for their wrongdoing. For centuries, humans have controlled one another by fear. The greater the fear, the greater the control. Yet, "An eye for an *eye,*" Grandfather said, "only makes the whole world blind."

THE WORD "ENEMY"

The word "enemy" does not exist in the vocabulary of nonviolence. Even the British, who ruthlessly captured, oppressed and exploited the people of India economically and politically, were not considered enemies.

UNDERSTANDING AND AGGRESSION

We generate conflicts when we have little or no respect for others, and when we are primarily concerned about our own desires and demands. We aggravate conflicts by injecting anger and aggression into our relationships rather than using our energy to find positive and equitable solutions. Learning to build and nurture good relationships with others, including those who challenge us, is a prerequisite to a nonviolent way of life.

A recent political situation in the southern United States, I believe, sheds light on this principle. I am referring to the widely publicized controversy over the use of the Confederate flag. The NAACP—the National Association for the Advancement of Colored People — has spearheaded for some years a nonviolent campaign to disallow any public display of the Confederate flag.

While they have succeeded in some places, they have created ill will in others. In Mississippi, for example, the feelings among whites and blacks over the issue escalated so high that it lead to a statewide political referendum, in which two thirds of the votes were cast in favor of retaining the Confederate flag.

I believe there were two things that went wrong in the NAACP's campaign. First, although the NAACP were not physically violent in their approach, they were very aggressive. Second, they lost sight of their ultimate purpose, which is to create and nurture harmony between whites and blacks in the United States. If the goal is to achieve true integration in the hearts of the people of the nation so that all can live with dignity and freedom, then aggressively fighting over a symbol is perhaps the wrong way to achieve it.

The issue of the Confederate flag seems to have only grown more bitter. Now that the die has been cast, the NAACP will have to take the battle to a new level, and the escalation could go on until one side or the other is legally restrained, or too tired to continue the fight. Neither of these outcomes will be a lasting victory.

PROACTIVE AND REACTIVE NONVIOLENCE

In order to operate successfully, nonviolence must be both proactive and reactive. Reactive nonviolence gained prominence through Grandfather and Dr. Martin Luther King Jr., who acted in response to the discrimination they encountered in their societies. Grandfather reacted first to the prejudices in South Africa, and later to British colonialism in India. Dr. King reacted to racism in the United States.

Grandfather's use of proactive nonviolence in South Africa and India received much less attention from the public. In its proactive mode nonviolence involves cultivating the sensibilities and compassion needed to respect others and their needs so that we can live in harmony. In South Africa, for example, while acting against discriminatory laws and practices nonviolently, Grandfather worked to improve everyday relationships between whites and nonwhites in order to avoid future conflicts. Similarly, in India he tried to improve relations between Hindus and Muslims, between high castes and low castes, between the rich and the poor.

According to Grandfather, the proactive mode of nonviolence involves "trusteeship," which means that, individually and collectively, we are trustees of the talents and resources that we have and not the owners. Our responsibility is to use them for the benefit of all.

In our selfish mode we consider ourselves owners of these things and, therefore, we exploit them for personal gain. This selfishness causes friction among people, leading eventually to conflict. If, however, we share our talents and resources intelligently, and help one other to attain our common and individual goals, we will create lasting peace.

THE FIVE ELEMENTS OF NONVIOLENCE

Whether used proactively or reactively, a fundamental principle of nonviolence is to bring about better relationships between the oppressed and the oppressor, through what I have sometimes described as "The Five Elements of Nonviolence": love, respect, understanding, acceptance and appreciation.

Gandhi and King succeeded in their objectives to a large degree by applying these elements. It would be a mistake to suppose that they were successful because they were contending with kind, compassionate or conscientious opposition. Ruthless attempts were made to crush their movements in India and in the United States, and both, ultimately, sacrificed their lives to their causes. Nevertheless, by their quiet, patient and sincere suffering in the face of gross injustice they both brought about deep and lasting transformation in their societies.

LAWS AND TRANSFORMATION

To outlaw discrimination and oppression, laws are necessary, but by no means sufficient. It is the nature of human beings to resent control by force. Any attempt to impose moral obligations upon unwilling people will lead to two reactions. The first will be "tolerance" by those who don't want to put up a fight. The second will be counter-aggression by those who resent forceful conversion.

For any law to be effective, Grandfather said, it must first have moral appeal. For the most part, people refrain from stealing not because they are afraid of breaking the law, but because they know it is morally wrong to take what does not belong to them. Many of the same people will ignore seat belt laws, because they attach no moral obligation to their observance.

When people are forced to respect civil rights and human rights or face legal consequences, they don't like it. Civil rights laws will be scrupulously observed only when people accept that it is morally wrong to oppress or discriminate against fellow human beings. That awareness can come only through education. A law will enable integration in public places, but it does not foster understanding or appreciation in the hearts of people who continue to live with their prejudices.

The only way, Grandfather concluded, to achieve respectful relationships is through the transformation of the heart. Violence and law are useless in this effort. "You can change people's hearts by love," he said, "never by law."

APPLE SEEDS AND ORANGES

The basis for Grandfather's belief in the philosophy of nonviolence lies in the Hindu conviction that all people are endowed with good and bad qualities. If we appeal to a person's bad qualities, then what emerges is conflict and violence and, on the other hand, if we appeal to good qualities, then what emerges is compassion and understanding. The proof of this can be seen every day.

When we yell or curse at someone, we get the same in return. On the other hand if we love and show compassion to even the most hard-hearted, he or she will ultimately respond with goodness. We cannot plant an apple seed and expect to reap oranges.

TOLERANCE

In recent decades we have emphasized the value of teaching people "tolerance." Tolerance is not only inadequate, it is a negative concept which only alienates society further. Learning to tolerate absolves people of the responsibility of learning to understand different people, accept and appreciate their differences, and progress towards respecting them for who and what they are. It is only when we build acceptance between people that we will rid ourselves of the scourge of prejudice and liberate ourselves from violence.

RESPECT FOR THE FAMILY

"If there is no respect for the family," Grandfather said, "there can be no respect for the society!' A society is only as loving and cohesive as its families. The family structure in modern times is going through a metamorphosis. Individuals are becoming more independent and more self-centered, because human life as a whole is tainted by materialism. Success is measured in terms of material possessions, and consequently, we teach our children to get to the top by any means possible.

In too many cases, marriages have become meaningless. Sex and materialism have become the most important aspects of life. To get a satisfactory dose of each, people are willing to break marriages and relationships easily. Raising a family was once the reason for two people to get married and stay married. Now many children are simply by-products of a sexual alliance.

In 1988, still new to the United States, my wife and I were given a ride by a young couple that was headed for a holiday. They were so ecstatic that we thought they were newly married and going on their honeymoon. We learned during the conversation that they had been married for five years and that they had a three-month old baby. They felt that they needed to get away from the baby and have some time for themselves.

"Oh, so you are among the lucky few who have a family to take care of the baby while you are on holiday," my wife, Sunanda, commented.

"No," said the lady. "The baby is with a nanny."

"Then, you are fortunate to have a nanny you know and trust to take care of your baby while you are away," Sunanda persisted.

"Well, in fact," said the lady, "we advertised for one and she was hired the day before we left."

To a couple of Easterners this was unthinkable. We have since heard parents talk openly of looking forward to the day when their children would grow up and leave the house so that they could have more time for their own lives. We *need* to reevaluate such attitudes if we are serious about building a strong society.

LEGACY OF LOVE

As we contemplate the world around us, it may seem that we have inherited a legacy of social injustice and domestic and international violence that has sunk to irretrievable depths. One may reasonably ask, "Will it ever be possible to build a world *free* of hate and prejudice?"

Grandfather's answer to this question could not be simpler or more sincere. "Change is possible if we have the desire and the commitment to make it happen."

We are surrounded by many things that were once considered to be impossible, things that we now take for granted. These things have become part of our lives because someone refused to accept the common wisdom. If this is possible in the material and technological sense, it is equally possible in the moral sense.

Grandfather said, "We must be the change we wish to see in the world." Beginning with ourselves, we must cause positive change to radiate out into the world. We need a change of heart, a change of perceptions, and a change of attitude, which we can then pass on to others through education, enlightenment and love.

Character, virtue, ethics—these concepts are getting more and more attention in education these days. In the past, there were three key institutions involved in raising the well-rounded child: the family, the school system, and a faith community. Fortunate are those kids who have solid support in each of these areas today. But as our society has evolved, we as parents need to become more intentional about what kind of people, what kind of human beings, what kind of members of society we want our children to become. We have to be more conscious and conscientious in helping learn to help guide them so that the can become capable, caring and successful individuals who can contribute to society.

In this piece Psychologist, **DR. RYAN M. NIEMIEC**, Education Director at the non-profit VIA Institute on Character, shows you how to indentify your child's core character strengths. And he gives us some good practical advice on how to help our children enhance them as well.

—Marc Sachnoff, Chief Parent, The Parents Union

CHARACTER STRENGTHS

BY RYAN M. NIEMIEC, PSY.D.

Education Director, VIA Institute on Character

© 2012, VIA Institute and Ryan Niemiec. www.viacharacter.org.

Used with permission.

Character is who we are. It is part of our positive personality. Our character strengths are what is best in us and help us express a sense of goodness into the world.

Our character is not something that is fixed and unchanging, and it doesn't boil down to just a few words. Instead, the latest science is discovering that character is "plural." We all have many character strengths that we can tap into at any given time. This is true for adults and children. In fact, we all have different amounts of at least 24 strengths of character. See page 27 (Chapter 2) for a chart on the VIA Classification of character strengths and virtues which outlines these qualities found in all human beings.

CHARACTER STRENGTHS: SEEDS YOU CAN NOURISH

Character strengths are capacities – or potentials within us – for thinking, feeling, and behaving in positive ways. We can consider the 24 strengths as seeds within us and within your child. If you place your attention on any of these 24 seeds in your child, the seeds may sprout and grow. Perhaps the seed will turn into a tall redwood tree, or maybe a beautiful apple tree? As parents, we cannot know for sure. What we can do is water these seeds and teach our children to water them as well. Point out the strengths you see in your child; encourage all of the strengths. Help the child discover which strengths are easiest to express. When you see your child express kindness, water it. When you see a flash of leadership or a tinge of creativity, water these. Your child will benefit and will be headed toward greater happiness and well-being.

How might you begin nourishing your child's strengths of goodness? Here are some ways you might approach your child. These give you ideas for immediate action you might take with your child's strengths of character. You might say something to them like:

- "Take a look at this list here [of the 24 character strengths]. What do you see as your highest character strengths?"
- "I noticed bravery in you yesterday. Did you see that too?"
- "I'm seeing curiosity in you right now. You are asking me lots of questions and you are exploring this topic really well. Nice use of your curiosity strength!"

- "Let's take this survey online to help identify your highest strengths? Then, we can discuss it and see if you agree with the results. Okay?"
- "Here are some pictures of kids doing activities that related to various strengths, which of these strengths do you connect with most?"
- "That really was a great movie, wasn't it? What do you think the main character's highest strengths were?"
- "Let's talk about your best qualities. How can you use them during this next activity?"

Example: Robert is a good father of a son with ADHD. He does the best he can to manage the challenges his son presents. Until he learned about the importance of character strengths, Robert had not realized he was spending all of his time focusing on his son's problems – difficulty getting homework done, talking back, and impulsive behavior. Robert was forgetting that, like every child, his son has many character strengths. There was so much more to his son than a diagnosis, yet he was only giving attention to negative behaviors. He was not watering his son's positive qualities. Upon realizing this, Robert began to point out, encourage, and express value for his son's character strengths – curiosity, creativity, fairness, love, and humility.

YOUR CHARACTER STRENGTHS ROAD-MAP

There are many ways you can help your child make the most of their character strengths. We all need some direction, or a "road map," at one point or another. The words "road-map" can serve as an acronym for ways that you model the use of strengths or help teach strengths to your child. Each of the following "action verbs" can be applied to any of the 24 character strengths in the VIA Classification.

- Reflect: Think about ways you have used strengths in your past successes and in your struggles.
- Observe: Take in your surroundings with your five senses. What strengths do you see in the interactions happening around you?
- Appreciate: Tell others about how you value their strengths. Name the strength that you see them express and share the specific rationale for how you saw them display the strength in action.
- Discuss: Communicate with others about your strengths. "Strengths of character" can be your topic of conversation with your family and friends.
- Monitor: Track your strengths use throughout the day. Set up a chart that helps you monitor what you are doing and where you are when you are using a particular strength.
- Ask: Get feedback from your family and friends on the strengths you use. What strengths do others see in you that you don't see?
- Plan: Set a goal or action plan for a strength you'd like to boost. Turn your use of strengths into a routine. You might wish to set up reminders or strengths cues using Post-It Notes.

The Value of Modeling

You are one of the most important role models in your child's life. Much of what your child learns will be gained through observation of you, and this occurs far more than we realize! Take time to explore this ripe learning opportunity with your child.

Who are you child's heroes, role models, and mentors? Who are the healthy people your child learns from? What are the character strengths that these individuals embody, embrace, and express? Remember to look far and wide for good, healthy models.

- Which family members and relatives are mentors? What are their highest strengths?
- Which teachers or coaches serve as a role model? What are their highest strengths?
- Which neighbors or friends act as good models for particular strengths?
- What characters from books does your child look up to? What are their highest strengths?

  Example: Harry Potter for his creativity and hope?

  Example: Katniss from The Hunger Games for her perseverance and love?
- What characters from movies are heroes to your child? What are their highest strengths?

  Example: Alice from Alice in Wonderland (2010) for her curiosity and honesty?

  Example: Nemo from Finding Nemo (2003) for bravery, love, and perseverance?

Summary: Key Things to Remember

- Use your own signature strengths. Identify your highest strengths of character (www.viame.org) and use them each day.
- The more that you are mindful of your own signature strengths, the better you will be at helping your child with their strengths.
- Put on a positive lens. Look for what is good in your child. It's OK to spot negative qualities as well, but it's highly beneficial for your child if the positives you spot outweigh the negatives.
- Research tidbit: Scientists have found that an optimal positivity ratio is about 3:1 (meaning that for every 1 negative comment or experience there should be 3 positive ones).

- Spot your child's strengths and give a rationale for what you saw.

  Example: On the basketball court, I observed you use such great perseverance because you never gave up, even when the team was losing by 15!

  Example: When you were playing with your friends the other day, I looked out the window and saw you helping a child who had fallen down. What a great use of kindness!

  Example: You did a nice job passing out those pieces of candy to everyone. It looks like you gave every child two pieces. You were using your fairness strength, weren't you?

- Help your child connect character strengths with their learning.

  Example: If the child is learning about Abraham Lincoln or Amelia Earhart, have a discussion about the character strengths of these important figures in history.

  Example: If the child is learning a new sport, discuss the value of the strengths of teamwork, leadership, and other character strengths you observe in the experience.

- When your child is struggling, ask them how they might call forth their strengths to help.

  Example: Suzie, I see that you are having difficulty with this math assignment, which of your best strengths might you use to help you in this situation?

  Example: Ben and Caleb, it looks like the two of you aren't getting along right now. How could each of you use one of your signature strengths so that you can start getting along better?

- New ways: Encourage your child to use their character strengths in new ways each day. This will help them feel more comfortable "in their own skin" and will likely provide a boost to their well-being.

  Example: For zest, do a new activity, sport, or hobby.

  Example: For kindness, look for a new way to help out another person such as holding the door for them or picking up something that has been dropped.

  Example: For humor, tell a silly story about something that happened to you in the last week.

15

CREATING A CULTURE OF LOVE OF LEARNING IN YOUR HOME

CAROL FRODGE has been a teacher, a principal and an education researcher. When we talked about some of the important things we as parents can do to help our kids succeed in school, Carol immediately replied, "We need to create a culture of 'love of learning' in our homes." We all want our children to succeed, and Carol's insights can help you take some easy steps toward making your home a place where learning is valued, shared and enjoyed.

—Marc Sachnoff, Chief Parent, The Parents Union

CREATING A CULTURE OF LOVE OF LEARNING IN YOUR HOME

BY CAROL FRODGE

The power of the culture of your home on how your child learns cannot be overestimated. The culture of learning in your home is formed by how you view and enjoy learning new things, whether you are a reader and how available printed materials are, and how much you engage one another in the enjoyment of learning.

Even in the best of schools, students experience setbacks and frustration. Success in school and beyond can be heavily influenced by an individual's resiliency, or the ability to "bounce back" from adversity. You can help your child develop resiliency.

Through the culture of learning you create in your home, you can provide the three protective factors for resiliency:

(1) caring relationships,

(2) positive and high expectations, and

(3) opportunities for meaningful participation.

(1) Caring Relationships

- **Be role models:** Children learn so much from watching others, particularly family members. If you openly show your own love of learning, it will be contagious. Be curious out loud. Include your child in your hobbies and interests as well as developing theirs. We learn best what we can physically experience. What we see and hear we can imitate and then adapt to fit our own style and interests.

  One of my children's friends told me a story about a great activity that she and her father did while they were waiting for an appointment. He has an interest in math and engineering and they decided to estimate the number of hairs on her head. He counted the number of hairs in a small section of her head and then had her look in a mirror and come up with a way to estimate the number of similar sized sections on her head. Then they did the multiplication. It was a very positive and fun way for him to share his love of math in an activity that involved her. It may seem like a small thing but it gave her an appreciation for estimation, an important concept in math.

- **Give feedback:** We all want to know how we are doing in the eyes of our loved ones. Give your children lots of specific feedback about their activities. Give them recognition when they do something particularly well or something thoughtful that you didn't expect.

- **Listening:** There is nothing more respectful than listening to your child's words or behaviors. Listen fully to what they are saying to you before you think of your response. Especially with younger children, their behaviors tell you more than the words they say. With behavior you have to think about what they are trying to tell you by their actions.

- **Conversation:** What and how we think is pretty much invisible. It's up to you to engage your child in conversation to help them verbalize their thinking. How you question your child can be instrumental in developing your relationship with them and in helping them develop thinking skills. Questioning takes 4 basic forms: What is it like? How does it work? How is this like something I have seen before? How do you know? The more you can use these different question forms, the more you will develop their thinking skills.

    There is a large body of research around the power of questioning. One very valuable resource is Project Zero at Harvard (see http://pzweb.harvard.edu/vt/Visible Thinking_html_files/VisibleThinking1.html). It is designed for educators, but it is also very useful for parents who want to develop a culture of thinking in their homes also.

(2) Positive and High Expectations

Having high expectations for your child and supporting them to reach meet those expectations is probably the single greatest factor that affects student achievement.

Positive and respectful relationship with school: Your child needs to know that you highly value the place where he/she spends the largest part of their day. Know your child's teacher and principal. Know the school's expectations and reinforce them at home. Constantly talk with your child about what they are learning in school.

Structure and rules at home: Provide clear rules and routines at home. Expect your child to follow them and have consistent positive rewards when rules are followed and highly predictable and consistent consequences when they are not. It is very powerful to have a conversation with them about what the rewards and consequences should be when you set up your rules. The rewards and consequences need to be meaningful to them.

Encourage autonomy: Adults, especially parents, who encourage the child to do things on her own and to seek help as needed, help the child to be autonomous. Praise your child when he or she shows initiative and autonomy, and help them, perhaps through practice or conversation, to do things independently.

Keep them thinking about the long view: Constantly tell your children that they are capable of going to college and that you expect them to go to college. You can help them frame what they are learning now for a long term goal. Students who believe from an early age that they are expected to go to college have a much higher likelihood of fulfilling that expectation.

(3) Opportunities for meaningful participation

Responsibilities at home: Everyone feels a sense of accomplishment with a job well done. Giving children jobs in your home that are age appropriate and that can be accomplished with little adult help will give your child an opportunity to develop a positive work ethic and a sense of responsibility to contribute to the success of the family. Below is a link to a site that has age appropriate chore lists. (Check out http://housekeeping.about.com/od/chorechart1/a/ageapprchores.htm)/

Lots of playtime: Through unstructured play children sharpen their imagination and develop critical problem-solving skills. It also teaches them to tolerate frustration. It also helps children learn that doing things again and again leads to improvement.

A great example of this is the Marshmallow Challenge. This is a problem solving challenge that is often given to groups of adults to help them develop group problem solving skills. In this challenge small groups are given a set selection of objects and they are to try to build the highest tower that can support a marshmallow at the top. It turns out that Kindergartners can build among the best structures because they know the value of trying again and again to improve the design. You can learn more about the Marshmallow Challenge at http://marshmallowchallenge.com/TED_Talk.html.

Develop a sense of " I Can": At every age, children need to become more confident about their ability to interact with others. They need to learn how to communicate, problem solve, manage their feelings and impulses, gauge the temperament of others, and seek trusting relationships. When you talk with them about a challenge they are experiencing, frame the conversation with what they "can" do. Have them voice, "I can …" and list their options.

RESOURCES:

http://resilnet.uiuc.edu/library/grotb95b.html#chapter1

http://cecp.air.org/familybriefs/docs/Resiliency1.pdf

http://www.naturalchild.org/jan_hunt/unschooling.html

http://www.wapirc.org/

http://fathers.com/

http://www.parenting.org/

16

BECOME AN ADVOCATE FOR ALL CHILDREN

MARY BERGSTROM is director of membership at The Parents Union and spent many years as a community organizer for various issues. In this piece, she shares a powerful method to help you bring together a group of parents around a specific problem by using story-telling techniques. Nothing is more powerful than a parent's authentic story. And when parents unite through shared stories, their impact on educators and policymakers can be profound.

—Marc Sachnoff, Chief Parent, The Parents Union

BECOME AN ADVOCATE FOR ALL CHILDREN

BY MARY BERGSTROM

Many years ago, I stood in a small circle of people gathered to practice "free speech" or "radical" action depending on your heart and viewpoint. Today, I still remember feeling that the flame of the candle that I held was there more to protect me from the hostility of those outside of the group than the frosty winter night.

Two young men stood taunting the small gathering of middle-aged men and women with a few "twentyish" persons sprinkled in between. Unable to provoke the group, they got louder and angrier and seemed on the verge of becoming physical.

But then a man with a pepper grey beard stepped out of the group and went to talk to them. For several minutes, their hands and arms waved around and their heads jerked up and down as they talked tensely to him. But gradually, you could feel a calm descending over the two young men. The man reached out and patted one on the shoulder. A few minutes later the two hugged each other before joining the group together while the other young man stood quietly to the side.

Over the next two decades, I was fortunate to have many opportunities to play a substantive role as an organizer, activist, and campaign leader for initiatives to establish environmental protections, against consumer fraud, for access to quality health care, and more.

Yet with each campaign and initiative and every passing year, I was left wondering. Why were we not more effective in the long term? Why were the hard won gains so often overturned or simply sputtered out? What was missing?

Every organizer knows that it is necessary to mobilize the very people with the problem or need that requires action. And it had always appeared to me that there was the buy-in and engagement of real people—the "grassroots" if you will. But with closer examination, I had to admit that such efforts were largely led by the same individuals each time—elected officials, policy experts and organizers—who were passionate and committed, but also professional activists. I had become one as well.

And that's why my mind goes back to this experience so many years ago. In that situation, one person truly listened to the story of another and by doing so, validated the feelings, created a personal connection, and identified the core values that united both of them. In this case, it was love of country and the right to personal expression.

And now, we at The Parents Union recognize that the strength of a movement and an organization is only as strong as its commitment to develop leadership. Because The Parents Union is an organization founded on values and not on policy, we are not held back by issue "silos" and instead see differences and diversity among people as an asset rather than obstacle.

Our organizing approach, the **Triad of Trust**, is a simple pathway from making the commitment to **personal engagement to empowerment to powerful**. Using this approach and the resources contained within this book, we feel confident that you can be part of a powerful movement that not only makes a world class education a reality for your child, but for every child. After all, YOU are The Parents Union.

Triad of Trust

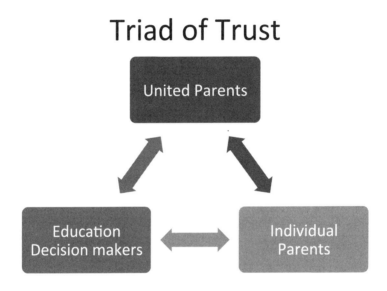

PERSONAL, EMPOWERED AND POWERFUL

First, leadership is **personal**. It begins with becoming the expert at telling your own story, conveying both the experience of it and the challenges and opportunities.

Next, because your story is "lived" experience, it resonates with feelings that can touch others with similar experience. This is the first step towards **empowerment**, as it moves us from isolation and its byproducts of self-doubt and immobilization to unity, hope, and shared commitment.

At this point, many of us might jump to identifying "issues" or solutions to the most pressing problems of individuals. But this would be a mistake.

Relationships based on person-to-person contact come first. Only in this way can stories be shared, compared, and most importantly, values in common identified.

Values are the sticky glue to building relationships among people. Because values are experienced emotionally, there is opportunity to break down barriers between persons and groups and allow for people to make real commitments to each other and take risks.

Finally, while **power** begins when one person to steps forward to tell his or her story (and, by doing so, unites others), to be truly powerful requires intentional and strategic thinking.

WINNING STRATEGY FOR POWERFUL PARENTS:

Stories That Bring People Together

As parent leaders, we must know each other before we can possibly know the issues. That means creating a connection of shared core values among all. As challenging as this sounds given differences in background, race, culture, language and more, it is only by doing that can we create a clear set of ground rules for decision-making, actions, and sense of community. For each of the parents within your group, consider the following:

- How would you describe the kind of person that you wish your child to become?

- How would you describe the type of life you wish your child to live as an adult?

- In what type of environment does your child thrive?

- How would you describe the kind of school environment and leadership necessary for your child to have the best education possible?

- In what environment does your child best learn?

- What hopes and dreams do you have for your child? What might he or she aspire to be?

As a group and when you compare your answers to these questions, what values do you find in common? Of these, what are the top three that you can agree upon? Are there others? Do they mean the same to each member of the group? If not, how might you further define them?

Once you have done the work to establish core values in common with all parent leaders in your group, it is also important to decide how you will represent these values. That is, how will each of you individually and as a group act?

It is good, at this point, to reaffirm the values through a technique exploring "moments of truth" for each value. The "moment of truth" comes when something is not right or even gone wrong. For example, if an issue is presented to a school leader with decisionmaking authority and the response is a solution that only benefits some members of your group, how will you respond?

The idea of these questions and undertaking this exercise is to stimulate conversation and create personal connection and cohesiveness within your group. It is worth making the investment in time to identify and solidify core values. This will allow for you to keep a sense of integrity, knowing what is right, and structure to decision making that instills confidence and clarity among your group.

STORIES TOLD WITH PURPOSE

The goal of our collective action is to achieve real change for real people—in this case parents and their families especially—that provides real value.

By value, we mean that change is aligned with the attributes that the group has defined for themselves, but also that improves the quality of life for those affected and in a way that is empowering.

To do this well requires applying a screen to identify issues or solutions to the problems surfaced by the group are seen as achieving these ends. In addition, these questions should be considered. Is or does the issue:

- Align with our values?

- Provide benefits to all if our efforts are successful?

- Easily understood by group members and for others that it affects?

- Have clearly stated goals and outcomes directed to specific individual decisionmakers?

- Give all members of the group the opportunity for meaningful roles and opportunities to develop leadership skills?

- Has a timeframe and level of effort required for which individuals will make commitments?

STORIES THAT ARE HEARD

Now that we have become expert at our individual stories and created a shared story and shared values, our stories must be heard to not just raise awareness, but to create change. For this to happen, we must do three things.

- Identify other parents and families who are also affected, determine how they are organized, and presenting ourselves in a way that personifies our values, we must engage them through the channels of communication that are most accessible.

- For each goal, we must identify the individuals who are charged with making decisions that will result in achievement of these goals. In addition and even more importantly, we must determine how we tangibly hold power over decisionmakers. Typically this is directly by the ability to vote for or against these individuals or to vote for or against persons who appoint them. Without doing this, our efforts will be diffuse and ineffective.

- Finally, we must identify "tactics" or activities that comfortably and appropriate engage our group and others who stand to benefit from our efforts. These tactics must effectively engage and persuade decision makers to stand with us and for us. Tactics must:
  - Personify the values of the group and come across as compelling and positive to the public and media.
  - Have a clear message and call to action.
  - Illustrate the power held by the group over the decision-maker and yet be within the comfort zone of and even inspire members of the group.

"To every story there belongs another," said Francisco DeGoya, the Spanish painter regarded both as the last of the Old Masters and first of the moderns. And we at The Parents Union believe that to every story belongs hope and opportunity for every child to master the skills for a whole and happy and successful life.

PARENTS' GUIDE TO SCHOOL BOARD ADVOCACY IN WASHINGTON

A project of the American Civil Liberties Union
of Washington Foundation

(reprinted with permission)

This is intended to serve as a tool for parents who want to communicate and advocate before their school board. *It is not meant to provide legal advice.*

For more information, please see the American Civil Liberties Union of Washington publications,

- **Parents' Guide to Public School Discipline in Washington**
- **Parents' Guide to Truancy in Washington, and**
- **Know Your Rights—A Guide for Public School Students in Washington**, available on our website: www.aclu-wa.org.

INTRODUCTION

School board members make important decisions that affect children's lives and education.

Under Washington law, children have a constitutionally guaranteed right to an education. They also have many other rights when they are in school. School boards set policies and make decisions on a wide range of issues that impact your child's rights, including what curricular and extra-curricular programs are available, how and when students are disciplined, and how the district's funds are spent.

School administrators, including the principal and superintendent, can help you resolve many issues that come up at school. But only the school board can approve changes to district policies or approve funding for new programs. Although superintendents and other school administrators cannot change policies, they can often be your strongest allies in advocating before the board.

This pamphlet provides a brief description of how school boards function and then guides you through some simple steps to make your voice heard. It can also help you prepare to raise concerns or make suggestions first with the principal or superintendent.

WHY IS SCHOOL BOARD ADVOCACY IMPORTANT?

The school board needs your experience and insight.

You can play an active role in setting policies by communicating your concerns and ideas to board members. School board members cannot be in the schools every day. They need to hear from students, parents and family members about what is working, what is not working, what services are needed, and what your priorities are for your child's education. Personal stories are powerful tools for change. School board members can learn from *your* story.

You can help protect your child's rights and find real solutions when problems arise.

Parents, working together with board members and school administrators, can come up with innovative solutions and create successful programs. These can include:

- creating after-school and tutoring programs
- designing effective and culturally relevant curriculum
- adopting policies that require parent contact before

police interview children at school
- improving communication with parents, including parents who do not speak English
- providing programs and training to make the school environment safe and welcoming for all students

HOW DO SCHOOL BOARDS FUNCTION?

The following is general information about how school boards function, including:

1. **Who are school board members?**
2. **What are school boards' duties?**
3. **How do school boards function?**

Remember, each school board may work a bit differently. **Be sure to contact your school district office to get the details on your board's members, meetings and policies!**

1. Who are school board members?

Every school district in Washington state is governed by an elected board of directors, commonly called a "school board." Most school boards are made up of five individuals who live within the school district and are elected by voters of the district. Districts serving large urban areas have seven elected board members.

2. What are school boards' duties?

School boards have the final say on a school district's policies and procedures, and on the district's budget.

District policies

Each school board adopts a set of policies that control its actions and provide standards for students and school staff. School board policies cover a variety of issues, including curriculum and grading systems, parent involvement plans, attendance, school discipline, harassment, freedom of expression, student records and student dress. Other policies relate to a district's internal operations, like hiring and firing, vacation time, building maintenance, and so on.

Get Involved!

In some cases, school boards are required to involve committees of various people in developing and reviewing district policies. Those committees often must include teachers, students, parents and community members.

Watch for public notices and listen for announcements at school board meetings for opportunities to get involved!

District procedures

Most school district policies are accompanied by related procedures. Procedures give detailed information about how a policy will be implemented in the schools. Many districts give the superintendent authority to develop the district's procedures. If your superintendent is responsible for drafting procedures, be sure to talk to the superintendent as well as the board.

Appeals in school discipline cases

Some school boards also hear appeals from individual student discipline cases. If you have a complaint about the discipline imposed on your child in a particular instance, you must follow the school district's formal steps in the grievance and appeal processes! You can find more information about these procedures in our *Parents' Guide to Public School Discipline in Washington*, available at our Web site: www.aclu-wa.org.

3. How do school boards function?

School boards, like other governmental bodies in Washington state, are governed by our state's Open Public Meetings Act.

Open public meetings

With few exceptions, the board must conduct its business in open public meetings. The board's business includes more than just the casting of final votes. It also includes the discussions between board members as they reach their decisions on how to vote.

Exceptions for privacy

School boards must also respect the privacy of individual students and of school personnel. School boards should not discuss the discipline of individual students in an open public meeting. They also will generally not discuss complaints about a particular district employee in an open public meeting.

Individual vs. General Concerns

Individual grievances will generally be heard in a closed session. Each district has procedures for handling student discipline hearings. Your board should also have a procedure that you can follow to bring up concerns about particular employees, generally in a closed session with the board.

If you are raising general concerns or suggestions regarding district policies, you should be able to present your ideas at an open school board meeting.

Public participation

The Open Public Meetings Act guarantees the public an opportunity to observe their elected representatives as they consider and make decisions. It does not give the public a right to speak at meetings. However, most school boards do allow members of the public to comment on agenda items at some point during their meetings. They may also allow members of the public to add new items to the agenda.

COMMUNICATING WITH THE SCHOOL BOARD

The next sections of this guide describe several steps that can help you effectively communicate your concerns to school board members in writing, or at a school board meeting. There are tips for:

- Writing to Your School Board Members
- Calling Your School Board Members
- Meeting with Your School Board Members

Careful preparation can help you make an effective presentation to the board. But if you have a concern, a question or a compliment, go ahead and get in touch with them. You do not have to be an expert on education policy, or have all the answers in advance. You can let the board members know that you are still exploring an issue.

Speak Up!

Do not be shy about calling your school board members or going to a board meeting! Remember that you have unique insights into what is happening with your child.

WRITING TO YOUR SCHOOL BOARD MEMBERS

Letters sent by mail or facsimile are an effective way of communicating with your school board members. Often a letter will be seen as representing not only the position of the writer, but also many other parents who did not take the time to write.

E-mail can be another effective way to communicate with school board members. Remember to be just as careful about what you write in an e-mail as you would in a letter.

If you prefer to write in a language other than English, check with the district office to see if they have someone who can translate your letter or e-mail for the board members.

Here are six tips for writing an effective letter or e-mail:

1. **Keep it brief:** Letters should never be longer than one page and should be limited to one issue. School board members often have separate full-time jobs and have a lot of reading material to go through before each meeting.

2. **State who you are and what you want up front:** In the first paragraph, tell your board members that you are a parent or family member of a child in their district. Identify the issue you are writing about. If your letter relates to a specific policy or procedure, identify it by its name and number.

3. **Hit your three most important points:** Choose the three strongest points that will be most effective in persuading your school board members to support your position and explain these to the board.

4. **Personalize your letter:** Tell your school board member why this policy matters in your community. If you have one, include a personal story that shows how this issue affects you and your family. **Do not underestimate the power of your own story. Personal stories have a strong impact.**

5. **Personalize your relationship:** Have you ever voted for the school board member? Are you familiar with him or her through any business or personal relationship? If so, say so.

6. **You are the expert:** Remember that the school board's job is to represent you. Be courteous and to the point, but do not be afraid to take a firm position. You may know more about the issue than the board member – this is your chance to educate him or her about the issue.

CALLING YOUR SCHOOL BOARD MEMBERS

You can also call school board members and let them know where you stand on the issues. If school board members find that their positions are unpopular, your call may contribute to a change in policy. If a board member asks you to put your concerns in writing, follow up with a brief letter.

If you will need an interpreter, call the district office to see if they can help you arrange to have an interpreter available on the phone or at an in-person meeting.

Back up a letter, e-mail or phone call with face-to-face communication at a school board meeting!

MEETING WITH YOUR SCHOOL BOARD MEMBERS

School board meetings are public, and speaking in public can be intimidating. But there are ways to overcome your fears and speak up for children.

- First, **remember that the board members work for you!**
- If you have never spoken at a school board meeting, you might want to **go to one or two meetings just to observe.** You can get a sense of the individual board members and watch how the board conducts its business.
- Try to **work with another parent or an organized group.** It can strengthen your message and give you more confidence.

You can always start by trying to set up individual meetings with board members to see where they stand on an issue. But you should also follow up by raising your issue at a school board meeting.

School boards are made up of at least five people, so if you have even one or two board members on your side, your presence at a school board meeting can help them gain the support of their fellow board members and the public.

The following sections include suggestions for:

1. **Preparing for a school board meeting**
2. **Making an effective presentation**
3. **Following up after the meeting**

Before you meet with your school board members, it is a good idea to check in with your principal and superintendent first.

Check in with your principal and superintendent!
Many districts have policies describing how parents and others can bring concerns and suggestions to the board.

If you have an individual complaint about a school staff member, the policies may require that you first raise your concerns with the principal and then the superintendent, before bringing them to the board.

If you are interested in changing an existing school policy or proposing a new program, your district's policy might encourage you to bring your ideas directly to the school board.

Remember!

There are specific rules that apply when you are challenging a specific disciplinary incident! For more information, look for our **Parents' Guide to Public School Discipline in Washington**, available at our Web site: www.aclu-wa.org.

To learn more about the steps for bringing concerns and ideas to your school board, call your district office and ask for the district's policies on public participation in board meetings or taking complaints from citizens. If your district's policies ask you to take concerns first to the principal, and then to the superintendent, you should follow those steps.

Even if your district's policy does not require it, talking to your principal and superintendent first can be a wise move.

Because many school boards rely on their superintendent's recommendations, you might find that the superintendent will be your strongest ally in advocating before the board. Also, superintendents are generally responsible for writing the procedures that implement the policies. It is important to talk with the superintendent in order to have input on how the procedures are written.

Follow Your District's Policies

Even if you expect that the principal or superintendent will not support your position, it is important to follow the steps set forth in your district's policy. Otherwise the board might turn you away for failing to follow their policy.

The principal might also support your position and be able to help you identify what policies already exist and how they might be improved.

The tips in the next sections also can be helpful in communicating effectively with your superintendent and other school administrators before you go to the board.

1. Preparing for a school board meeting

Request time on the agenda

Contact the district office to find out how to get on the agenda for one of the board's monthly meetings. Let them know what issue and policy, by name and number if you can, you wish to discuss. Make sure they know that you are a parent or family member of a child in their district.

If you will need an interpreter, contact the district office as far in advance as possible to see if they can make someone available.

Look at the district's policies and procedures

Find out whether there is already a policy and procedure in place that addresses your issue. You can look in your parent/student handbook or ask your principal or superintendent. You can also look through the district's policy manual yourself.

Some school districts have their policies and procedures available on their Web sites. If not, ask the district office where you can find a hard copy of the policy manual.

Translations: If you need a translation of a policy or procedure, call the district office to ask if they have copies in your language or can provide an interpreter to translate them for you.

If a policy or procedure addresses your issue, review it to see if it seems reasonable and if it is being followed properly by the district.

Find out about your rights relating to the issue

Information about students' and parents' rights can be found in parent/student handbooks, district policies and procedures, and in the ACLU of Washington's guides, available on our Web site: www. aclu-wa.org:

- **Parents' Guide to Public School Discipline in Washington,**
- **Parents' Guide to Truancy in Washington,** and
- **Know Your Rights—A Guide for Public School Students in Washington**

Gather information

If you are asking the school board to support a new program, try to gather information about "best practices." If you know people in nearby or similar districts with programs that are working, be ready to describe them to the board and recommend people the board can contact for more information.

Also, if you have access to the Internet, you can find a variety of reports describing successful programs and problem-solving approaches in schools.

Washington State Report Card Web Site

For information on academic testing results, teaching staff, budget and student demographics for your district and school and how they compare to others, you can go to the Washington State Report Card Web site at: http://reportcard.ospi.k12.wa.us/.

Connect with other parents and families

What do others in your community think? Work with other parents, families and students to define the problem and discuss possible solutions. Think about who your allies might be in seeking the change you want.

You might find support from existing parent groups, teachers or community leaders.

Think about the big picture and anticipate objections

When you decide to bring an issue to the school board, it will usually be because it affects your child. As you prepare, however, remember to consider how the change you are proposing would affect all children in the district. School board members are charged with making decisions that will be in the interest of the entire district and are often concerned with how a change will affect the district's budget.

One or more school board members may have already taken a position on the issue. Talk to others to learn more about your board members' views. Try to anticipate what reasons school board members, school administrators or other community members might have to oppose your position and be ready to answer them.

Recruit others to attend

If you are going to a school board meeting, bring along as many other parents, students and community members as you can! Not everyone needs to speak; just being there will let the board members know you care. Plan a carpool, share child care responsibilities or meet for dinner ahead of time so you can all make it there together.

If you have set up an individual meeting with a board member, bringing more than four or five people can be hard to manage. Keep it small, and bring people who represent different groups that have an interest in the issue. Let the board member know ahead of time how many people will attend the meeting.

Decide what you want to achieve
Make a clear outline of what changes you want to see. What is it you want the school board to do – vote for or against a policy? Make a commitment to introduce a new program or better support an existing one? Asking the school board to do something specific will help you know how successful your visit has been!

Agree on what to say
It is tough to make a strong case for your position when you are disagreeing with other members of your group during the meeting! Identify your most important points – these can be your "talking points." If a point is causing tension within your group, leave it out of your presentation to the board.

Lay out the plan for the meeting
People can get nervous in a meeting and time is limited. Be sure that you lay out the plan for presenting your issues beforehand, including who will speak first and what you will say in closing. Designate someone to talk and a different person to take notes.

Checklist: Preparing for a School Board Meeting

☐ Request time on the agenda
☐ Look at the district's policies and procedures

☐ Find out about your rights
☐ Gather information
☐ Connect with other parents and families
☐ Think about the big picture and anticipate objections
☐ Recruit others to attend
☐ Decide what you want to achieve
☐ Agree on what to say
☐ Lay out the plan for the meeting

2. Making an effective presentation

Be prompt and patient

At some school board meetings, you must arrive on time to get on the agenda to speak. School board meetings can run long. If you did not get added to the agenda ahead of time, be ready to wait until the end of the meeting to present your issue.

If you have arranged an individual meeting with a school board member, remember many of them have separate full-time jobs. Be sure to show up on time and be patient – it is not uncommon for meetings to run late.

Keep it short and focused!

You may have only a few minutes to present your concerns. Make the most of that brief time by sticking to your topic. Start by introducing yourselves and thanking the board members for taking the time to hear from you.

Effective Speaking

- Make it easy for people to hear you by standing and speaking clearly and distinctly.
- Keep focused on the board members, and make eye contact with them.

Stick to your talking points

Follow a prepared outline so you will be sure to hit your most important points. Stay on topic, and back your points up with no more than five pages of materials that you can leave with the board members. If you can, bring copies for each board member. Otherwise, you can give one to the Chair or President of the board and request that he or she distribute copies to the others.

Provide personal examples of the impact of the policy!

This is the most important thing you can do in the presentation. When you are telling your story, it is okay to be nervous and emotional—people understand that parents and families feel very strongly about the lives and education of their children.

If you get emotional, try to take a few deep breaths, and focus on a written outline to get you through your points.

Remember to always be respectful

Showing respect toward the board members, school administrators and other people in the audience—even if you disagree with their positions—will make it more likely that your concerns will be heard and taken seriously.

If a board member or other person is responding in anger, do your best to keep your cool and see if you can find points of agreement. Review the things you do agree on—including that you all want to figure out what will work best for the students—and try to narrow down your points of disagreement.

Realize that one of the keys for resolving conflicts is to allow people the time and information to consider your point of view.

If the board is reluctant to support the change you are seeking, you can ask them to explain their reasons and offer to provide additional information to support your position.

Saying "I don't know" can be a smart move

You do not need to be an expert on the topic you are discussing.

If you do not know the answer to a question, it is fine to tell the board members that you can get additional information for them. This gives you the chance to put your strongest arguments on the table and allows you to contact them again about the issue.

Never make up an answer to a question—giving wrong or inaccurate information can seriously damage your credibility!

Brainstorming Solutions

Remember, you do not need to have a solution in mind before you talk with your school board members. You can let them know that you are raising an issue because you want to work with them to brainstorm ideas about how to resolve it.

Confirm a plan for going forward

If the board is not going to act immediately, ask them what their next steps will be and request that they set a date when the issue will be on the agenda again.

Often, if a board member has not taken a position on a policy, he or she will not commit to one in the middle of a meeting. The board members may want time to consider a new proposal and research the potential impact on the district. They may also want to put the issue on the agenda for a future meeting to give other members of the public a chance to comment.

Checklist: Making an Effective Presentation

- ☐ Be prompt and patient
- ☐ Keep it short and focused
- ☐ Stick to your talking points
- ☐ Speak clearly and distinctly
- ☐ Provide personal examples
- ☐ Be respectful
- ☐ Offer to follow up with additional information
- ☐ Confirm a plan for going forward

3. Following up after the meeting

Review and reflect

Right after the meeting, compare notes with everyone in your group to understand what the board has committed to do and what followup information you committed to send. If a board member took the time to meet with you individually, each person who took part in the meeting should promptly send a personal thank you note.

Follow up in a timely fashion

If you need to get information to your school board member, set a clear timeline for when this will happen. If a board member has promised to get back to you, follow up with them. Be flexible, but persistent.

CONCLUSION

Remember—you can impact the policies that shape your child's education!

Your school board members need your experience, ideas and expertise to make sure your children are getting the education they are guaranteed by our state's constitution. When problems arise, you can help find real solutions to the issues facing your children in school.

By speaking up, you can be a powerful advocate for your child's rights!

Reprinted by permission:
The American Civil Liberties Union of Washington Foundation is the legal, research, and educational arm of the American Civil Liberties Union of Washington, a nonprofit, nonpartisan mem-

bership organization devoted to protecting and extending the civil liberties of all people in Washington.

American Civil Liberties Union Of Washington Foundation
705 2nd Avenue, 3rd Fl., Seattle, WA 98104
www.aclu–wa.org

VAUGHNETTA BARTON, executive director for the Foundation for Early Learning, has more than twenty years of service in the non-profit sector. Prior to joining the Foundation as director of programs in July 2007, Vaughnetta served in programs, communications, and development positions at organizations including Philanthropy Northwest, Big Brothers Big Sisters of Puget Sound, and Watermark Credit Union.

MARY BERGSTROM joined The Parents Union as director of membership in November 2011. Trained in organizational coaching and several organizing models including Midwest Academy's Direct Action Organizing, Mary Bergstrom has twenty-five years of experience and expertise in creating and leading public awareness and advocacy campaigns at the state, regional, and national levels for public benefit organizations including AARP.

WILLARD R. DAGGETT, Ed. D., founder and chairman of the International Center for Leadership in Education, is recognized worldwide for his proven ability to move preK–12 education systems toward more rigorous and relevant skills and knowledge for all students.

CHRISTOPHER EIDE is the co-founder and executive director of Teachers United, an organization of extraordinary educators who will change the face of public education. Teachers United operates under the belief that informed and empowered teachers should lead the way in sharing and improving classroom instruction and advocating for policies that promote an equitable and innovative system that puts students first. Chris was a classroom teacher for five years in high-poverty traditional and charter schools in Houston, New York City, and Seattle. He has also done national research on charter and transformation schools, lectured and produced workshops on mathematics instruction, and observed schools and instruction in more than twenty countries. Chris also holds a variety of leadership roles including founding board director of The Parents Union, executive committee member of the British-American Project, and the steering committees of Democrats For Education Reform-Washington and the Excellent Schools Now coalition.

JOYCE L. EPSTEIN, Ph.D., is director of the Center on School, Family, and Community Partnerships and the National Network of Partnership Schools, principal research scientist, and research professor of sociology at Johns Hopkins University.

BEVERLY FALGIONE is chief development officer at Easter Seals Washington and lead academic coach at A PLUS Youth Program.

ALINA FRANK has been consistently rated the top EFT coach since 2009. Aside from her private coaching practice in Seattle and Whidbey Island, Alina has been training and mentoring EFT practitioners internationally as a trainer of trainers since 2006.

CAROL FRODGE, M.S., has been a math and science teacher and school administrator for more than twenty-five years in Washington state and Ghana, West Africa. She is a board member of NW PBIS (Positive Behavioral Interventions and Supports).

ARUN GANDHI, born in 1934 in Durban, South Africa, is the fifth grandson of India's legendary leader, Mohandas K. "Mahatma" Gandhi. For the past five years, he has participated in the Renaissance Weekend deliberations with President Clinton and other well-respected Rhodes Scholars.

MARGERY B. GINSBERG, Ph.D., is an associate professor in the College of Education at the University of Washington. Her teaching and research interests are intrinsic motivation as the foundation of school and organizational renewal, culturally responsive teaching, adult learning, and leadership preparation.

HOWARD GLASSER, M.A., is the founder of the Children's Success Foundation and creator of the Nurtured Heart Approach™ and the Inner Wealth Initiative™, which have been used in hundreds of thousands of homes and classrooms around the world. He is the author of *Transforming the Difficult Child*, currently the top-selling book on the topic of ADHD (attention deficit hyperactivity disorder).

PHYLLIS HARVEY currently works with the University of Washington in the Office of Minority Affairs & Diversity as curriculum director for K–12, with Washington Mathematics Engineering and Science Achievement (MESA).

BRYAN C. HASSEL is an expert on education issues such as charter schools, school turnarounds, education entrepreneurship and human capital in education and co-director of Public Impact, a national education policy and management consulting firm based in Chapel Hill, North Carolina.

ANNE T. HENDERSON is a senior consultant with the Annenberg Institute for School Reform in Washington, D.C. As a leading authority about the relationship between families and schools, Anne has written many articles and books including *Beyond the Bake Sale: The Essential Guide to Family/School Partnerships.*

ERIN JONES has been involved in education for the past twenty years as an athletic coach, a public and private school teacher, an instructional coach, a state assistant superintendent, and a district executive. Erin has taught in a variety of environments, from predominantly African American to predominantly Caucasian to some of the most diverse communities in the nation. Erin received an award as the Most Innovative Foreign Language Teacher in 2007 and was the Washington State Milken Educator of the Year in 2008. Erin's greatest passion is to create equity by closing opportunity gaps and ensuring all students have access to quality early childhood programs, quality educators, high standards, culturally relevant curriculum, proportional access to special programs, and intentional instruction in academic English.

ALFIE KOHN writes and speaks widely on human behavior, education, and parenting. Kohn has been described in *Time* magazine as "perhaps the country's most outspoken critic of education's fixation on grades [and] test scores."

YAFFA MARITZ has a master's in clinical psychology and is a licensed mental health counselor with advanced training in infant mental health. She is an advocate on behalf of children and their families and serves on several local and national boards that promote this agenda, including the Governor's Commission for Child Abuse and Neglect Prevention.

JOE NEWMAN: Forty years ago, Joe Newman, M.A.O.M., was the "behavior problem" child. Defiant, difficult to control, physically aggressive and unable to sit still, in 1970 he was diagnosed with attention deficit hyperactivity disorder (ADHD) and put on Ritalin. Joe studied communication dynamics, conflict resolution, motivation and systems of interaction and received his master's degree in organizational management. Since 2004, Joe Newman has supervised and trained Behavior Specialists at the Kayne-Eras Center/Exceptional Children's Foundation in Culver City, California. Prior to that, Newman was the founder and director of Z-Wave, a mentoring program in Los Angeles, Chicago, Houston, San Diego, and Miami. He worked as an elementary and high school teacher, a crisis intervention specialist, and a director of education and curriculum. Today he trains parents, teachers, and behavior specialists in the powerful methods outlined in his book *Raising Lions* to heal behavior problem children.

RYAN M. NIEMIEC, Ph.D., is an author, licensed psychologist, and educator. He is education director of the VIA Institute on Character (www.viacharacter.org), a nonprofit organization in Cincinnati where he leads workshops training practitioners around the world on the science and practice of character strengths. Ryan is co-author of *Positive Psychology at the Movies: Using Films to Build Virtues and Character Strengths* (2008), *Movies and Mental Illness* (2005, 2010), and a number of book chapters and articles. He's associate editor of the journal *PsycCRITIQUES*, consulting editor for the *Journal of Popular Media Culture*, and chair of the Media Watch Committee for the American Psychological Association. In 2011, he received the Distinguished Early Career award from APA's media psychology division. His latest book, *Mindfulness and Character Strengths*, will be released in spring 2013.

JULIE ROSS, M.A., is the executive director of Parenting Horizons (www.parentinghorizons.com), an organization devoted to enriching children's lives through parent and teacher education. She is the author of *How to Hug a Porcupine: Negotiating the Prickly Points of the Tween Years*, in which she offers techniques for optimal parent to tween communication. Her other books include Practical Parenting *for the 21st Century: The Manual You Wish Had Come with Your Child, Joint Custody with a Jerk: Raising a Child with an Uncooperative Ex*, and *Now What Do I Do?: A Guide to Raising Elementary Aged Children*. Ms. Ross has led parenting workshops nationwide. In New York City, she frequently works with Parents in Action, The Parents League, The Board of Jewish Education, the New York City Public School system, and several private schools. Julie Ross is currently a member of the American Counseling Association and runs ongoing parent workshops and support groups.

BETH SIGALL is an education policy advisor and writer currently focused on education policy in Washington state. She is a court-appointed special advocate for foster children in the Juvenile/Dependency Court system in King County and is active in her school's parent teacher association, serving as the legislative and advocacy chairperson. Prior to working in the education policy arena, Beth practiced law as a special education attorney. She is the mother of three wonderful children, ages 13, 11 and 6.

INDEX

www.theparentsunion.org
www.facebook.com/TheParentsUnion
twitter.com/TheParentsUnion

*Mobilizing a united movement of parents and concerned citizens
toward the achievement of a world class education for every child.*